TRADING 101

TRADING 101

HOW TO TRADE LIKE A PRO

SUNNY J. HARRIS

John Wiley & Sons, Inc.
NEW YORK • CHICHESTER • BRISBANE • TORONTO • SINGAPORE

Copyright © 1996 by Sunny J. Harris
Published by John Wiley & Sons, Inc.

Library of Congress Cataloging-in-Publication Data:
Harris, Sunny J.
    Trading 101 : how to trade like a pro / Sunny J. Harris.
      p. cm.
    Includes bibliographical references and index.
    ISBN 0-471-14445-2 (cloth: alk.paper)
      1. Futures—Handbooks, manuals, etc. 2. Options (Finance)—
Handbooks, manuals, etc. 3. Futures—Data processing—Handbooks,
manuals, etc. 4. Options (Finance)—Data processing—Handbooks,
manuals, etc. I. Title.
  HG6024.A3H37 1996
  332.64'5—dc20   96-10258

Printed in the United States of America
10 9 8 7 6 5 4 3 2 1

This book is dedicated to my partner Gina L. Maraio who has stood by me and maintained the faith through thick and thin, to my daughter, Colby E. Littlejohn, who is my pride and joy, as well as my understudy and right-hand woman, and to my mother, Mae B. Evans, whose strength I emulate. Above all, I thank Howard*, Who is the inspiration and guidance in all that I do.

*From the children's prayer "Our Father Who art in Heaven, Howard be Thy name "

Well done is better than well said.

—Benjamin Franklin, *Poor Richard's Almanack*, 1737

Winners look for solutions—losers look for excuses.

—Adrienne Laris Toghraie

CONTENTS

Contents

FOREWORD

The beginning stages of a trader's education sets the foundation for each new level of success. The level of success you achieve is determined by your application of a good education. *Trading 101* gives a new trader the guidelines for developing the education necessary to begin trading.

Working as a traders' coach for the last six years, I have found that most excessive trading losses result from the bad habits traders develop at the beginning of their trading career. Some of these bad habits are created because a trader does not have:

1. the basic fundamental knowledge of the trading industry and how all of its components interrelate
2. a trading plan
3. rules they believe will give them good results
4. a tested system
5. money management rules

Lack of discipline is the main reason traders fail. In order to be disciplined you must trust your methodology and money management rules. If you have not developed the basic education necessary to be a good trader, you will not have the discipline necessary to follow your rules. If you do not follow your rules you will not get profitable results. *Trading 101* will give you the education you need so you can trust your ability as a trader.

The five main reasons beginning traders do not start out with the basics needed for good trading are:

1. Their enthusiasm to trade immediately takes over without giving thought to the possible consequences.
2. They do not know where to get the right information to start.
3. They find the method taught too difficult to understand.
4. They have information from too many sources which causes them to go in too many directions at the same time.
5. They feel that to succeed they must establish complicated rules which results in too many possible things that can go wrong.

Trading 101 is easy to understand, easy to apply quickly and will leave you with the confidence that you have the ability and knowledge to be a successful trader.

Sunny Harris is an extraordinary trader who was ranked the number one money manager in 1994 by Stark Research in the under $10,000,000 category. She won that honor trading a system she developed which could only be for the kind of trader who can look death in the face and laugh. This system brought in 365 percent last year on investment dollars, and fits the dynamo side of her personality. The second system she trades, which was also developed by her, is for traders with a pulse. This system brings in a very respectable, predictable and safe 18 percent with 8.5 percent drawdown. This system satisfies the conservative side of her. Recently, Sunny decided to make these two systems available to a limited number of traders who want to jumpstart their careers, but in order to be eligible for consideration, the trader must have the right personality type to bring out each system's best potential.

In addition to trading, Sunny publishes the *Traders' Catalog & Resource Guide.* She began this publicaton when it became general knowledge in the industry that she had been keeping a "black book" of sorts on everyone and everything in the business - from brokerages to software and weather. The word spread so far and wide about her "black book" that she was getting calls from all over the country. By April 1993, Sunny was putting together her first catalog. And that is how a great business idea was born.

While *TC&RG* is the phone book directory combined with editorial magazine, *Trading 101* is the cookbook. *TC&RG* is an alphabetical listing of who's who. *Trading 101* is the step-by-step guide you need to get started.

There is a lot to be learned from the brilliant investing and trading successes of Sunny Harris. Her determination, her thoroughness and her dedication to the techniques of trading and investing are an inspiration to all of us. And, there is also a lot to be learned from her willingness to organize and catalog the entire world of trading and to share it with the rest of us.

Trading 101 will give you the basic understanding of the trading business. It will save you time, money and research providing you with what is necessary to get started. *Trading 101* will be a continuous resource as you develop into a successful trader.

Sunny Harris' generosity to the investment world is a model of prosperity consciousness in action. Everyone seeking affluence in every part of their lives should follow her prosperity principle: "You only have what you give."

—Adrienne Laris Toghraie
April, 1996

PREFACE

I am now a professional trader. I was not always a trader, nor did I plan to become a trader. I was not an economist or a broker, or a banker or any other professional involved in the markets. I, like most other individual traders, came from a background unrelated to investing and trading.

In my *Trading 101* seminars, I always ask about my students' backgrounds and have found that many aspiring traders come from engineering, physics and mathematics backgrounds, as do I. It seems to me a natural extension of logical abilities, but does not mean that one has to have a degree in math to be a trader. Yet a solid foundation of logical abilities does seem to me an absolute necessity for developing a theory, thoroughly testing the theory, and following the trading system once developed.

My formal education has been in mathematics. As a new mathematician straight out of graduate school, I abhorred the thought of using my training for any practical application like programming. But, earning a living became a necessity, and I began programming in the aerospace industry. I quickly came to love the challenge and the opportunity to apply symbolic logic to "the real world".

After an immensely successful entrepreneurial venture into computer graphics, I began the process of learning how to invest my own money. Early on I bought stocks and bonds, I hired money managers, I ventured into mutual funds and money market funds, I purchased real estate, and a variety of limited partnerships. Most of these ventures were profitable, some very much so. At one point I lost $75,000 with a "sure thing" commodites trader and swore I'd never have anything to do with futures trading again.

While my advisors invested my money, I monitored the efficacy of their advice by keeping data and charts on a weekly basis. The mechanics of this process taught me the basics of technical analysis, and I wanted to learn more.

At first I kept my charts by hand on a piece of 10x10 graph paper, and I got my data from *Investors Business Daily* and the *Wall Street Journal* each morning. Later I began watching *FNN, the Financial News Network*, from 6:00am each morning until the market closed at 1:15pm California time.

The more I learned, the more I wanted to learn. I bought my first book on technical analysis, John Murphy's *Technical Analysis of the Futures Markets*, and dug in. After weeks of study, the pages of the book were nearly covered with flourescent yellow from highlighting, so I purchased a second copy and studied some more.

The more I studied, the more I feared that there was so much to learn that I had better leave money management to the professionals. But I was still curious.

As I kept my investment charts, I began keeping track of additional background charts: the Dow Jones Industrial Average, the dividends of the Dow, interest rates, and the price of gold. It was in this process that I began to see patterns, and to understand some of the concepts in John Murphy's work.

Initially, I observed that a parabolic curve usually collapses and that the dividend of the Dow tends to range between 3.0 and 6.0 and that the trend turns when the dividend stays too long at one extreme. In September of 1987 I saw these two conditions in the DJIA and decided to act. With over a million dollars in equities and equity funds, I told my broker to liquidate. He disagreed. "This is the biggest bull-run in history," he said. After a long lunch, at which I showed him my new-found technical analysis techniques, he still disagreed. Nevertheless, it was my money, so I liquidated and went to Europe on vacation.

When the market closed down 105 points on Friday, October 16, 1987, I stated firmly, "It'll drop 500 points on Monday. I can see it in the charts." From my hotel room in London I watched with excitement as the US market collapsed on that fateful Black Monday. I decided then and there to pursue advanced education in technical analysis—vigilantly.

Over the next 2 years I consumed books, audio and video tapes on technical analysis. I attended every seminar I could find which even remotely touched on technical analysis. I voraciously read newsletters and watched FNN religiously. As I studied, I kept notes, and vowed to one day write a book so that other novices would not have to go through the same gruelling process to learn about trading.

—Sunny J. Harris
April, 1996

1 GETTING STARTED

Introduction

This book, *Trading 101*, is the collection of years of study and experimentation, condensed to an easy-to-use guide for the newcomer. *Trading 101* is like an overview class: you will learn about the existence of concepts, but will not learn the concepts in depth. You will, however, learn where to look for information on each of these concepts, so that you may explore in-depth and develop your knowledge base further if a particular topic appeals to you. I've drawn liberally from the work of others, using quotes and telling you where you can find more information on each subject.

Trading 101 could have been subtitled "Everything You Ever Wanted to Know About Trading But Were Afraid to Ask," because we'll be covering many very basic questions (and their answers) that students are often afraid to ask in a large class for fear of asking "dumb questions."

There are thousands of professional money managers in the world: bankers, stock brokers, insurance brokers, real estate agents, art dealers, coin dealers, antique dealers, accountants, attorneys, and so on. Any one of these professionals will be happy to tell you that his (whenever I use the masculine pronoun I use it generically, implying his/her throughout this book) specialty is the only one which will stead you well for the long-term outlook. In other words, they're all salesmen. Each of these professionals has one goal foremost: to increase his own take-home pay.

There is no such thing as altruism. We all have personal motives for doing good deeds, whether it be attention getting, reward seeking, or monetary gain. For instance, I'm not writing this book just for kicks and because I want to see you make a lot of money—I'm writing it so you'll purchase the book, and as an aside I'm writing about a subject that I believe will assist you in making a lot of money. This is a trade: I get something of value and you get something of value. That's what this whole book is about, trading: the perceived fair exchange of one item or service for another item or service in the hopes that both parties benefit.

Trading 101 is not for the aforementioned professionals—they already know it all. This book is written for everyone else. I'll show you the ropes, pulling from many different resources. And I'll introduce you to concepts that you may want to study in-depth.

The Market

The market goes up and the market goes down. That's about all there is to it. Your job, as a trader, is to catch those swings at just the right time and price to profit from the movement.

Throughout this book, the word market will refer to anything that one person wants to buy and another person wants to sell. If I have a car that I want to sell and you want to purchase, then that's the market.

The action of negotiating for the price at which we are willing to complete this transaction is called **trading**. Trading, when it involves more than two people, is an **auction** process.

Definition:

Auction
A public sale of items to the highest bidders.

What Is Trading?

Trading is bartering; it is the exchange of goods or services. Trading has been part of human existence since the beginning of time. In fact, trading is truly the world's oldest profession. (Eve traded the apple for the knowledge of good and evil, didn't she?) Trading is not gambling, although some gamblers do trade.

Trading takes place when one person agrees to take the other person's eggs in exchange for vegetables. It happens when one barters two cows for a parcel of land. Trading also happens when you exchange coins for food. Each trader has a commodity that he perceives to have a value. The exchange takes place when the two parties agree that the value of each side of the trade is in parity.

If two traders do not agree that their commodities are of equal value, they will negotiate the quantities to be exchanged, until such time as they both are comfortable that the amounts to be traded are in parity. For instance, the trader with the land might want three cows to execute the trade, while the owner of the cows believes the land is only worth one cow. In this case, there is a spread between the bid and the ask prices.

The trader with the cows is only willing to bid one cow, while the trader with the land is asking three cows. There is a spread of two cows.

Definitions:

Bid:
An offer to purchase something at a specified price. The bid price is the highest price any buyer is prepared to pay.

Ask:
An offer to sell something at a specified price. The asking price is the lowest price at which any seller is prepared to sell.

Spread:
The difference between the asking price and the bid price.

Ultimately, if the trade is to take place, the two traders will negotiate, until one of them increases the bid or lowers the ask price.

As time goes on, and word gets around that these traders meet at a particular location to exchange wares, other people interested in bartering show up. Soon, we have a market place. In one town it might be the cheese market, in another the fish market, but there is always the exchange of one commodity for another commodity taking place.

The life of the early trader became complicated. In order to supply his needs, he found himself traveling from home with his cow, to the grain market where he traded his cow for more grain than he needed, on to the fish market where he traded part of the grain for some fish, and then to the egg market where he traded some more of the grain for some eggs, and then back home again with his grain, fish, and eggs. After some more negotiating with his friends and neighbors, they agreed to create a derivative, that would make their lives easier. Thus, currency was born.

Definition:

Derivative
A financial contract which does not necessarily have value of its own, but whose perceived value is based on the value of the underlying instrument(s).

The early traders were able to take their currency to market, negotiate the amount of currency to trade for the grain, the fish and the eggs, and return home. The currency did not need a value of its own. It was only necessary that all trading parties agree to make the trade based on the perceived underlying value of the currency.

The currency we use today in the United States is valueless. We carry around small pieces of paper with numbers on them and trade them at markets for other commodities which we want at the time. The trader on the other side of the trade agrees to take the piece of paper because he believes that it can be used in another market to make an exchange with someone else. The piece of paper itself does not have a value—only a perceived value.

Since our currency is no longer backed by gold or silver, you are no longer guaranteed the exchange of that paper for a fixed quantity of gold or silver. If a substantial number of traders began to doubt the value of the piece of paper, it would quickly become a worthless derivative. This same effect can happen with any derivative—traders can lose confidence in its value and the price will plummet. But for as long as we agree to bid and ask, trading will continue.

With each trade, the participants analyze their individual risk. Systematic traders will have analyzed the risk and measured it against the possible reward statistically. Discretionary (intuitive) traders will have measured their gut reaction to the impending trade.

Animals in nature trade without words. One animal kills the prey and allows several others to feed with him. The alpha animals will snarl and growl at animals it doesn't want to trade with and the opposing animal must weigh the risk of confronting the alpha animal versus the reward of eating the food.

Definition:

Risk/Reward Ratio
The relationship between the probability of loss and that of profit.

For instance, if you must put down $1,000 to make $500, the risk is pretty high. But if you can put down $1,000 to make $10,000, it looks pretty good.

HOWEVER, you must consider the probability of winning, before you actually know anything. What if, in the first example, the probability of winning is 50 percent, that is for every two trades, one of them wins. But in the second example, where you could win $10,000 the probability of winning is 1 percent. Would that be worth it?

In Chapter 15 we'll take a closer look at the way you figure this out.

Why Do You Want To Trade?

Excuses

The excitement.

Few endeavors challenge the excitement of putting your own money at risk. Las Vegas and Atlantic City will attest to this. Before we invented currencies, we risked life and limb to prove strength and courage. The Masai still expect young men to battle a lion as a rite of passage.

Nowadays we make more sophisticated wagers, betting our hard-earned dollars at football games, horse races and gaming tables. We revel in the excitement. We jump up and down and cheer for our side of the wager. Adrenaline surges through our bodies, our hearts pump faster. We love it!

This excitement can be extended to the investing arena. In fact, it is often true that losing can be more exciting than winning. The adrenaline high becomes its own reward. The determination to beat the market offers a challenge like no other.

The challenge.

Demonstrating your prowess, like fighting the lion, is a personal quest designed to cull the weak from the strong in the survival of the fittest game. It's part of our nature as humans to compete. We are designed to respond to the fight or flight adrenaline rush, but in modern times have very few outlets for this response.

The markets are the combined demonstration of thousands of competitors entering into an anonymous fight for profit. The waves of price movement in the markets are the aftermath of a sometimes fiercely competitive auction. Bid and ask prices are simply evidence of two opposing parties arguing about how much something should cost.

The challenge for a trader then becomes one of outsmarting the market. Novice and seasoned traders alike enter the game believing they can predict the next price move, and using the skills they bring to the arena (whether it be mathematics, intuition, science, psychology, or logic) attempt to buy or sell at a price that has not yet been reached.

If you are interested in trading the markets for the challenge, find something else to do. Take your hunger for challenge and play backgammon or chess or football. Challenge the bully up the street to a fist fight. But, forget about trading. Doing it for the challenge will lose your money.

The market is always right. You will not outsmart it—not consistently and over time. Eighty percent of the people who begin to trade the market today will not be trading in 12 months. And they didn't quit because they were wise and took their profits to the bank. Eighty percent of the traders lost their money to the twenty percent who trade with one consistent goal: **to make money**. This is the only goal that matters in trading.

Reasons

There is only one reason to trade: to make money. If you are trading the markets for any other reason, stop! Any other goal is simply an excuse to enter into the perceived excitement of the game.

Trading for the thrill is not a rational choice, and is usually short-lived, because losing money generates just as much an adrenaline rush as making money. Trading without a business plan, without a clear-cut system, can be fun, but dangerously costly.

The business of trading is boring if it's done right. The research and study, the testing and retesting of ideas, the consistent and unwavering following of your system does not create an adrenaline rush. The hard work and accomplishment does produce a feeling of satisfaction, when you have adhered to your rules over a long period of time and produced consistent results. You have a right to be proud of your work. But, you'll recognize when you are doing it correctly by the conspicuous absence of stress and adrenaline.

Learning the Jargon

Every field has its own set of buzz words that the participants in that endeavor all seem to know and the people outside the field don't know. The only way I know to get acquainted with a new language is by total immersion. Reading the definitions in the glossary of this book will help you start learning key words and their meanings. Take time each day to read this glossary again and again, in the same way a child learns a new language. Practice and repetition will speed the process along.

When I first began trading I had difficulty grasping the concept that you could sell something you didn't own. It took repetition and acceptance for me to catch onto the concept of selling something short.

Adages

Old adages and wives tales often have some basis in fact. In trading there are many sayings which float around year after year, such as:

- Buy low, sell high
- Let your profits run
- Take small losses
- Never let a win turn into a loss
- The trend is your friend
- Add to a winner, never to a loser
- When in doubt, get out

Some of these sayings are very true and should be posted on little yellow stickies beside your computer monitor. Some, however, couldn't be further from the truth. The only way to learn which adages are useful for you is to test. Test your theories to exhaustion and then follow your system. For instance, my system lets some winners turn into losses. That's the way the system works. If I were to try to second-guess the system I would create a lot of small losses and a lot of <u>small</u> wins! Traders usually depend on small losses and big wins, so in this case the adage doesn't apply.

"When in doubt, get out" is another erroneous adage. You'll always be in doubt! Trading takes discipline and nerves of steel. The only way to circumvent this natural emotion is to only trade a system that has been thoroughly tested and proven.

There are many more words of wisdom which traders of all kinds will be willing to share with you. Don't believe them. Don't believe anything until you have tested it. (See Chapter 15)

The most important adages for you to remember go like this:

- Anything that sounds too good to be true, usually is.
- There is no such thing as a free lunch.
- You get what you pay for.

Remember to invest in your education. You wouldn't wake up one morning and say "Today I'm a surgeon." You don't have the training for it. Why would you wake up one morning and say that you're a trader without the training?

For some strange reason, people throw their money at the markets without training and sufficient study. It has been observed that 80-90 percent of the people who begin trading today, will have lost all their trading capital within the first 12 months, and will quit trading. I think I know who they are. They're the ones without a proven system.

Remember, when you begin trading that you are pitting yourself against the pros. They are there to take your money. And they will do it quickly unless you have prepared yourself as well as they have. You're stepping into the ring with the world heavyweight champion!

The Exchanges

Definition:

Exchange
Association of persons engaged in the business of buying and selling stocks, futures and/or options.

There are more than 140 financial exchanges around the world, some large and some very small. As a beginner, let's stick with the main U.S. exchanges:

- New York Stock Exchange (NYSE)
- New York Futures Exchange (NYFE)
- New York Mercantile Exchange (NYME)
- Chicago Mercantile Exchange (CME)
- Chicago Board of Trade (CBT)
- Chicago Board Options Exchange (CBOE)
- Kansas City Board of Trade (KCBT)
- International Monetary Market (IMM)

- Commodity Exchange Corporation (CEC)
- Minneapolis Grain Exchange (MGE)

The New York Stock Exchange had its beginnings in 1792 where 24 merchants and auctioneers met outdoors under a buttonwood tree on Wall Street. Older countries than ours had cheese markets, flower markets, gold markets, spice markets and the like, which had specific gathering places and times at which to auction their wares. These were all exchanges.

Traditionally, trading takes place in pits.

Definition:

Pit
A specially constructed arena (usually circular) on the trading floor of exchanges where trading is conducted. Some exchanges call these area rings rather than pits. (See Figure 1.1)

Pits are usually constructed with risers, making the inside ring lower than the outside rings, so that people on the outermost edge can see over the people standing in front of them. What appears to be pandemonium is really an open outcry auction taking place, with the sale going to the highest bidder and purchased from the lowest offerer. Supply and demand determine prices, sort of. Actually fear and greed determine prices. When

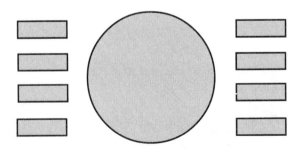

Figure 1.1   The Pit

people all want something that someone else has, it is greed that drives prices up. Conversely, when people are afraid of something losing its perceived value, they all try to get rid of it, at cheaper and cheaper prices. Successful trading takes into account the mathematics of human emotion.

Around the pits are banks of trading posts and telephones, where various firms locate their floor brokers. These floor brokers use hand signals to let the people in the pit know what they want to trade and for how much. The folks in the pit signal back when the deal is made, relaying the price at which the transaction took place. After each deal, a reporter places specially marked cards into a reporting device which records the transaction and causes it to appear on the ticker almost instantly.

Reading the Ticker Tape

While ticker tapes were once a long strip of paper coming out of a bubble shaped device (one of the many inventions of Alexander Graham Bell), for the most part they are all now digital electronics. Nevertheless, we still call it a tape. (See Figure 1.2)

Each trade that takes place in the pits is echoed on the tape in shorthand, with its corresponding ticker symbol, the price at which the transaction happened, and how many shares were traded. Stock trades which take place in multiples of 100 shares are called **round-lots**. Stock trades which are not multiples of 100 shares are called **odd-lots**.

Even though all these transactions are recorded on huge, state-of-the-art computers, the verbal auction sometimes takes place faster than the clerks can report them. Then we say that the market got ahead of the tape. In fact, the clerks are just behind in their paperwork. If all trading

Figure 1.2   The Ticker Tape

took place electronically, rather than in open outcry auctions, the market could not get ahead of the tape.

In the Appendix you'll find a list of exchanges with products available at each, and a table showing specifications for some of these products.

Margin

Definition:

> **Margin**
>
> In stock trading, an account in which purchase of stock may be financed with borrowed money; in futures trading, the deposit placed with the clearinghouse to assure fulfillment of the contract. This amount varies daily and is settled in cash.

In stock trading, you may borrow up to half the price of the stock, usually against your account's total value, so that you may buy more stock than you could with cash only. For instance, if shares of XYZ stock are $100 each, you would pay $10,000 cash for 100 shares. If you margined the stock at 50 percent, you purchase 200 shares for the same $10,000.

The added leverage is to your benefit if the stock moves in your favor: you'll make twice the profit. However, if the stock moves against you, you'll have twice the loss.

Using margin is like buying a house with credit. You put down 20 percent of the price of the house, the bank loans you the rest.

If housing prices decline and you have to sell your house, you'll still have to pay off the bank, even if your house sells for less than you paid for it. Even if your house burns down, you'll still have to pay off the bank. But if housing prices rise before you sell your house, the profit you realize will be measured against your down payment, not against the full price of the house, so you make a higher rate of return.

This relationship is even more evident in futures trading, where the margin requirements are much lower. For instance, if the S&P 500 Index is trading at 400 it means that one share each of 500 stocks times the index value of 400 gives a current value of $200,000 for the index. Yet, at current margin levels, you can trade one contract with a $12,000 margin deposit. That's only a 6 percent margin requirement. If you purchase a contract and the value goes up, your profit is measured against your initial margin, a larger percentage than if you had paid cash. Again, if the contract decreases in value, you've lost a greater percentage than if you had paid cash. And in the unlikely event that the S&P dropped to zero, you'd be responsible for the full $200,000.

When determining whether or not to use margin, you must evaluate the risk versus the reward. I look at worst cases when evaluating risk. What is the worst percentage drop the market has ever had? From a high of about 380 in 1929 to a low of about 40 in 1932 is almost a 90 percent drop. From a high of roughly 2600 to a low of roughly 1900 in 1987 is just about a 27 percent drop. Then I would look at the probability of the worst case happening. How many times in history has the market experienced a decline of more than 27 percent? What is the  average decline? How often do declines of this size take place? Only after I understand the risk do I begin to evaluate reward strategies.

Further Reading

For a light look at the basics of getting started, read *The Wall Street Journal Guide to Understanding Money & Markets*. For specific information about exchanges and exchange products, write or call the exchanges themselves. (See Appendix for numbers.)

In *The New Contrarian Investment Strategy*, David Dreman does a fantastic job of giving an overview of and introduction to trading. Published in 1980, this book is as true today as it was then. Dreman's common sense, practical approach makes this book must reading for beginners.

Wiley publishes a "Getting Started" series of books, each of which is an A-to-Z primer that will give you a jump start on the learning process: *Getting Started in Futures* by Todd Lofton and *Getting Started in Options* by Michael C. Thomsett.

2 APPROACHES

Fundamental Analysis

The analytical method by which only the sales, earnings and the value of a given tradable's assets may be considered is called **fundamental analysis**. The theory holds that stock market activity may be predicted by looking at the relative data and statistics of a stock as well as the management of the company in question and its earnings.

Fundamental analysis relies on the study of reports to predict price trends; it addresses what a stock *should* sell for. In trading stocks, for instance, fundamental analysts rely on quarterly earnings reports; they look at reports about the company's products and personnel; they study reports about that sector of the economy and that industry in general.

To my mind, these are all just reports generated by humans striving to create a picture that satisfies their boss, or the board of directors, or their stockholders. I've been on boards of directors. I know what happens in those meetings. That's why I rely strictly on technical analysis.

Quoting from Steven Achelis in *Technical Analysis from A to Z*:

If we were all totally logical and could separate our emotions from our investment decisions, then fundamental analysis, the determination of price based on futures earnings, would work magnificently. And since we would all have the same completely logical expectations, prices would change only when quarterly reports or relevant news was released.

Fundamental analysts study other trading vehicles in addition to stocks. Fundamentalists trade commodities, currencies and interest rates as well. Some futures contracts move according to fundamental information. Soybean crops are affected by rain and lack of rain; the price of pigs and cows is affected by the price of their feed.

So, let's cover the fundamental analysis topics and see where we can find the information we would need as fundamental analysts.

Economic Indicators

There are eight statistics professional fundamental analysts regularly watch.

- **Leading Indicators** This monthly composite of 12 indicators is released by the Commerce Department's Bureau of Economic Analysis. Some believe that this index shows where the economy will be six months from now. The S&P 500 index is itself one of the leading indicators. Others include housing starts and orders for business equipment.
- **Real GDP** (Gross Domestic Product, formerly Gross National Product) The Commerce Department releases both projections and retrospective numbers for each quarter's inflation-adjusted GDP.
- **Unemployment**
- **Labor Costs** One measure is the employment cost index, which is calculated quarterly by the Bureau of Labor Statistics and reported in the *Wall Street Journal*.
- **Productivity** Hourly worker productivity affects inflation. When productivity is improving, companies can afford to pay their workers more without having to recover it all through price increases.
- **Inventory** If sales fail to materialize excess inventory has to be reduced, companies will buy fewer new items, thereby slowing

the economy. The Commerce Department issues a ratio in the middle of each month comparing the dollar value of business inventory nationally with sales.

- **The Dollar** A strong dollar encourages cheap imports, holding inflation down but hurting certain U.S. industries that depend upon exporting. A weakening dollar helps U.S. manufacturers, but may encourage inflation.

- **Interest Rates** The Federal Reserve tries to push rates down to stimulate the economy and raise them when it is growing too fast. The Fed puts its policy into effect chiefly by setting the level of short-term interest rates. When short-term rates are higher than long-term rates, it means the Fed is trying to slow business activity; when short-term rates are lower, the Fed is trying to speed up the economy.

Pick up a copy of *Money Guide-The Stock Market*. Michael Sivy writes several of the chapters in this informative and basic book on investing, and it is well worth reading.

Analysis of Economic Data

Basic rules of thumb are kind of like adages, they work sometimes. As with any theory, my advice to you is always "test it!" That said, the following table gives you a quick start for fundamental analysis that includes economic indicators.

Activity	Anticipated Direction of the Market
Fed Raises Discount Rate	
An increase in the borrowing rate for banks usually results in increased rates for customers. Slows credit expansion.	
Money Supply Increases	
Excess money supply growth potentially can cause inflation and generate fears the Fed may tighten money growth by allowing Fed funds rates to rise which, in turn, lowers futures prices.	

Fed Does Repurchase Agreement ↑

Fed puts money into banking system by purchasing collateral and agreeing to resell later. This helps bring rates down.

Fed Does Reverses or Matched Sales ↓

Fed takes money from the system by selling collateral and agreeing to repurchase at a later date. This decrease in money supply generally raises interest rates.

Fed Buys Bills ↑

Fed permanently adds to banking system reserves which may cause interest rates to drop.

Consumer Price Index Rises ↓

Rising inflation.

Durable Goods Orders Rise ↓

Pickup in business activity usually leads to increased credit demand.

Gross Domestic Product Falls ↑

Slowing economy. Fed may loosen money supply prompting decline in interest rates.

Housing Starts Rise ↓

Growth in economy and increased credit demand. Fed less accommodating and may attempt tightening by allowing rates to rise.

Industrial Production Falls ↑

Slowing economy. Fed may allow interest rates to fall to stimulate economy.

Inventories Up ↑

Slowing economy since sales not keeping up with production.

Leading Indicators Up ↓

Strength in economy leading to greater credit demand.

Oil Prices Fall ↑

Reduces upward pressure on interest rates, enhancing prices of debt securities.

Personal Income Rises ↓

Higher income equals more consumption, which equals increased demand and higher prices for consumer goods.

Precious Metals Prices Fall	↑
Decreased inflation. Demand for inflation hedges abates.	
Producer Price Index Rises	↓
Rising inflation. Demand for goods rises as well as prices. Investors require higher rates of return, pushing rates up.	
Retail Rates Rise	↓
Stronger economic growth. Fed may have to tighten.	
Unemployment Rises	↑
Slow economic growth. Fed may ease credit, causing rate to drop.	

Sources of Fundamental Data

Investor's Business Daily (IBD) frequently runs a section called Investor's *NewsWire*. While this section is actually advertorial in nature, it is devoted to corporate announcements. In Section A *IBD* supplies Earnings News, New Issues, and psychological data. Section B of *IBD* covers "The Economy" and includes reports on economic data and corporate news.

Most of the on-line services provide both historical information and projections on fundamental data. We'll use *America OnLine (AOL)* here, for illustration, but you should look in Chapter 3 for information on other important online services.

From the Main Menu of AOL you can click on [Business] and from there link to *Business Week* or *Investors Business Daily*. Or you can click on [Company Research] which provides stock reports (from Morningstar), financial statements (by Disclosure), earnings estimates (by FirstCall), and Edgars 10Ks and 10Qs (by Disclosure)

Again from the Business section of AOL, you can click on [Market News] which leads to stock market details, international markets, commodities, money and currencies and economic indicators.

There are government related bulletin board services which supply fundamental data. Chapter 3 helps you find some of those.

What Should You Read?

Take a look at *Theory and Problems of Principles of Economics* by Dominick Salvatore and Eugene A. Diulio, if you want a quick overview of fundamentals. This book is straight forward and uses the Schaum's Outline Series format, right to the point without a lot of verbiage.

For a more in-depth study of fundamentals, I suggest *Economic Analysis-Theory and Application* by S. Charles Maurice et al.

If you look at these books and balk at the amount of work you're going to have to do to become a trader, find another profession. This is not a quick and easy process; it takes years of study and devotion. When you put your money on the line, you'll be competing with professional traders who have spent their lives learning how to trade. Don't show up unprepared.

Technical Analysis

Technical Analysis is the study of prices. Technical analysts study supply and demand for securities and commodities based on trading price and volume. Using charts and modeling techniques, technicians attempt to identify price trends in a market. (See Figure 2.1)

My research leads me to believe that all the information I'll ever need is in price. The price of the underlying instrument already reflects

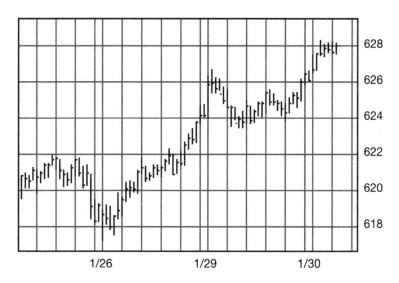

Figure 2.1   A chart is worth a thousand numbers.

opinion, rumor, volume, volatility, news, and fundamentals, before it ever gets to my computer screen.

Generally technical analysts use charts of price to learn about price behavior and price patterns, but this is not always so. Some great technical analysts never look at a chart, but rather do their analysis on the numbers alone.

Consider the following list of prices: 619.50, 620.10, 620.20, 620.10, 621.05, 621.30, 620.65, 620.80, 621.30, 621.10, 621.30, 621.65.

Do you see anything? I don't.

How about that old adage "a chart is worth a thousand numbers"?

The number sequence above is found in the center of the chart in figure 2.1. Now I can see several things: an uptrend, a range, a trend line, and a bounce. Whether you chart by hand or using a computer, technical analysis is easier with a picture.

Time Frames

The time frame in which you trade will be determined by several factors. First and foremost, what's your day job? How do you support yourself while you are learning to be a successful trader? If you are retired and independently wealthy, you can trade in any timeframe you like; if you work from nine to five, then you had better trade with end-of-day data in a longer time frame than if you could watch the market minute-by-minute all day long.

Secondly, what is your nature? Are you an adrenaline junkie who drinks lots of coffee and can't wait for the next challenge, or are you mellow and prefer a life of relaxation and no hassles?

Next you must consider the nature of the market you want to trade. Each market has its own rhythm. Some markets ask to be traded intra-day and often, some reveal only a few good trades each year.

Long-Term vs. Short-Term

Beginning traders often want to know just exactly how many days or months constitute long-term. To me, these words are both relative. Long-term in my personal trading is about three days. If I hold a position that long, it is approaching a record length trade in my system. Yet, if I were a bond trader and made trades weekly instead of hourly, long-term would be a matter of months. In real estate ventures what's long-term? Years.

Nevertheless, to most people long-term seems to mean months to years, intermediate-term is weeks to months, and short-term is hours to weeks.

Real-Time vs. End-of-Day Data

Let's answer the easier question first. **End-of-day data** is based on the closing price for the day. You may collect your data daily or weekly or historically, but if it includes closing prices for the day, and not prices during the day, then it's end-of-day data. You can get this data from many vendors as well as from online services. (See the Appendix). Usually you'll download it into your  computer over a modem, or read it in from diskette. Some vendors have their own BBSs from which you can purchase end-of-day data, and some even have special transmitters that send the data to you over an FM radio signal or through your Cable-TV signals.

Real-time data is data you receive while it's happening. The only delay you should experience in this data is the amount of time it takes to transmit to and from the satellite—just a few seconds. Of course, this is in an ideal world. Practically speaking, there is the additional delay of data entry on the floor of the exchange. When things get hectic in fast moving markets, the data entry clerks can't keep up with the transactions as fast as they happen. Then even a real-time data feed will fall behind what's really happening on the floor. And when the market is moving really,  really fast it's next to impossible to get your phone call through to your broker as well. That's when I step aside; I can't trade without data, so I get out of the market until the data is once again available on a real-time basis.

To receive real-time data you need a special receiver that connects to your computer, and a vendor to transmit the data to you. In addition, you need permission from each exchange to receive their data and of course this means you'll pay the exchange a fee for that permission.

Real-time, end-of-day and delayed data are transmitted to you by several means. You can get data with a modem, transmitted over the phone lines into your computer. Data is available through your local cable TV. Data is also transmitted by satellite and over the FM radio waves. Contact each data vendor about the methods they use.

3 SOURCES OF INFORMATION AND DATA

Introduction

Nowhere is the adage "you get what you pay for" more true than in the acquisition of data. Your trading decisions are directly influenced by the accuracy of your data. If you think you'll save money by collecting your own data, or finding a free source on the Internet or paying some discounted price for shareware, FORGET IT. And don't trade data with your buddies.

The money you lose by making bad decisions with bad data will far outweigh any savings you made on the purchase of cheap data. As with any business tool, buy the best you can afford.

You are trading to make money. This is a business. You are a capitalist. As a capitalist you must pay for the goods and services you receive, to keep other capitalists providing those goods and services. This business is market driven, like the software business. If you pay someone to do good work, they'll do it; otherwise you'll be whining that you have bad data and can't make good trading decisions. Data is available somewhere on almost anything. The data must be input and maintained by someone, and you'll get what you pay for.

Bulletin Boards

Bulletin Board Services (BBS) are often small enterprises maintained (loosely) by a single individual. Some, on the other hand, are corporate or government in nature and have financial backing. Many of the small BBS come and go within weeks or months. Frequently your local weekly computer rag will list other BBS numbers in the back.

Often BBSs will maintain collections of information which you can download for free. This can be a way to get started and to discover if you enjoy the process of research before you begin trading. Data acquired for free should not be relied on to make trading decisions, but can be a useful practice tool.

In the Appendix you'll find a list of financially oriented bulletin board services. Explore them with your mind open to discovering more questions than answers, which will often lead your imagination down unexplored paths.

Chart Services

If you don't have, or don't want to get, your own computer and data, fear not. You can still do a tremendous amount of technical analysis of charts that others have produced for you. Charting services sometimes fax you, but more often mail you charts of almost any and all stocks and commodities. You can get long-term and short-term charts on a daily, weekly, or monthly basis. Most of these services overlay the charts with a moving average  or sometimes additional technical indicators, and usually show volume, price/earnings ratios, yields, dividends, and shares outstanding.

Commodity Trend Service of Palm Beach Gardens, FL, (800) 331-1069, provides chart books for futures, futures options, long-term charts, and nightly fax chart services.

Knight-Ridder Financial of Chicago, IL, (800) 537-9617, provides a wealth of weekly and monthly chart services, as well as long-term publications like *Encyclopedia of Historical Charts*, *Commodity Perspective*, *CRB Commodity Yearbook*, and *Megatech Wall Charts*.

M.C. Horsey & Company, Inc. of Salisbury, MD, (410) 742-3700 publishes *The Stock Picture* six times per year with 10 charts per page, 204 pages.

Mansfield Stock Chart Service of Jersey City, NJ, (201) 795-0629, publishes *OTC I, OTC II* and *OTC III* weekly with 9 charts per page, 267 pages.

Oster Communications of Cedar Falls, IA, (319) 277-1271, publishes *Commodity Price Charts*.

Securities Research Company of Wellesley Hills, MA, (617) 235-0900, publishes Security Charts, Wall Charts, OTC Charts (short- and long-term), 35-Year Charts, Century Charts, Cycli-Graphs and more on a quarterly basis.

The Value Line Investment Survey provides over 2,000 pages of information on stocks, including a long-term chart at the top of each page. Their information is fundamental in nature, but still provides a comprehensive long-term view of each stock. This tome is published by Value Line Publishing, Inc. of New York, NY, (800) 624-3583.

William O'Neil Co. of Los Angeles, CA, (310) 448-6843, provides *Daily Graphs*. These are the *Investor's Business Daily* publishers, which, by the way, is also an excellent chart service in itself and probably the least expensive way to go. Just pick up a copy at the newsstand and you're on your way.

Commercial Data Vendors

- **Bonneville Market Information (BMI)**
  (800) 255-7374
  BMI offers over 110,000 real-time and delayed quotes on equities, bonds, futures, options, mutual funds and indices, along with a variety of informative news and weather services through FM, cable, and satellite services.

- **Commodity Systems, Inc. (CSI)**
  (800) 274-4727
  CSI provides daily updates and historical data on commodities, stocks, options, indexes and mutual funds.

- **Data Broadcasting Corp. (DBC)**
  (800) 527-0722 x719
  DBC is the nation's leader in providing real-time market data to the individual investor. DBC transmits quotes on over 65,000 stocks, options, and commodities. The Signal receiver brings quotes to your PC via FM, cable or satellite.

- **Data Transmission Network Corp. (DTN)**
  (800) 475-4755 x361G
  DTN offers 15-minute delayed quotes on stocks and bonds, real-time index quotes, as well as quotes on mutual funds, futures, precious metals, and a business news service.

- **Dial /Data**
  (718) 522-6886
  Since 1972 leading institutional investors and thousands of individuals have relied on Dial/Data for its industry-standard database of daily and historical securities prices for U.S., Canadian, European, and Pacific Rim exchange-traded equities, futures, equity options, mutual funds, bonds, government issues, money markets, indices, and stock dividends.

- **Genesis Financial Data Services**
  (800) 808-3282
  Genesis offers two data packages: historical data from 1968 on 140+ commodities and historical data from 1970 on 8000 stocks. With the package you get their Navigator data management software which allows you to convert the data between more than 20 formats.

- **Pinnacle Data Corp.**
  (800) 724-4903
  Pinnacle specializes in hard-to-find historical data. With their free communications software you can download index and breadth data, continuous futures contracts, and commitment of trader reports.

- **Prophet Information Services Inc.**
  (800) 772-8040
  Prophet gives you historical data back to 1968, customized updating capability, high-speed modem access, and a vast selection of stocks and futures from around the world.

- **Stock Data Corp.**
  (410) 280-5533
  Stock Data has historical data by diskette or modem for the NYSE, AMEX, and NASDAQ.
- **Telerate Systems, Inc.**
  (201) 938-4000
  Telerate offers dial-up modem access to their global information network.
- **Telescan, Inc.**
  (800) 324-8246
  Telescan has current and historical quotes on stocks, mutual funds, indexes, and options, which you can import to spreadsheet and charting programs.
- **Tick Data, Inc.**
  (800) 822-8425
  Tick Data has historical data on a tick-by-tick or daily basis. They also have a dial-up end-of-day updating service for both the daily and tick data.

Magazines

For the most part magazines are not a source of timely trading data. It takes six weeks to publish and mail a magazine, and therefore the data is stale by the time it gets to you. Nevertheless, there are a few pieces of valuable data to be gleaned from the following magazines:

Technical Analysis of Stocks and Commodities publishes a table of

Trading Liquidity for Futures, that is essential to you as a trader in this respect: if the market you're trading is not liquid you will be stuck on the wrong side of a trade at some point and not be able to get out. My advise to you is: only trade markets with high liquidity.

Futures magazine publishes a calendar that is a source of fundamental data, of a sort. Contract expirations, economic reports, and earnings reports can effect short-term price fluctuations. If you want to know when these events are about to happen, check the calendar in the back of *Futures*.

In the same magazine you can usually find a table of data comparing the performance of top CTAs (Commodity Trading Advisors) and CPOs (Commodity Pool Operators). If you're looking for someone to manage your money, start your quest by checking *Futures'* "Managed Money Review."

While you don't really find data in magazines, you will find advertisements for companies that will sell you data. Magazine ads are, in fact, your way of staying in touch with the leading edge of technology. When a new data service emerges, it will be advertising its wares.

Newspapers

Barron's is a weekly publication of Dow Jones & Company, Inc., (800) 328-6800, appearing in the format all newspapers should adopt: it folds out like a big magazine so you can read it on the train or airplane with someone sitting next to you. The Market Week section of *Barron's* is chock full of data on stocks (U.S. and Foreign), bonds, mutual finds, closed-end funds, money market funds, variable annuities, options, stock indices, futures, economic indicators, and charts.

In addition to the enormous variety of other information *Consensus—National Futures and Financial Weekly* published by Consensus, Inc. of Kansas City, MO, (816) 471-3862, provides comprehensive charting of all actively traded futures.

Investor's Business Daily, (800) 831-2525, published daily except weekends and holidays is the most data-oriented newspaper. IBD starts right out with tables of data: Amex, bonds, credit markets, dividends, earnings, futures, industry groups, markets charts, money rates, mutual funds, Nasdaq OTC, national markets, new highs & lows, new issues, NYSE, options and world markets.

The Wall Street Journal, (800) JOURNAL, also a publication of Dow Jones & Company, Inc., is published daily except for weekends and holidays. This one you need a big desk for, but the Money and Investing section gives you daily data on money rates, municipal bonds, mutual funds, stocks, new issues, bonds, NYSE highs and lows, odd lot trading, program trading, treasury issues, regional markets, and world markets. For 95 cents per minute you can call their 900 number (1-900-JOURNAL) to get news updates and current quotes.

On-Line Services

Each of the on-line services offers a wide variety of data, some free (except for the price of your membership to the service), some for a fee.

The main subscription/membership on-line services are:

- **America On-Line (AOL)**
  8619 Westwood Center Dr., Vienna, VA • (800) 827-6364
- **CompuServe**
  5000 Arlington Center Blvd., Columbus, OH • (614) 457-8600
- **Dow Jones**
  PO Box 300, Princeton. NJ • (800) 815-5100
- **GEnie**
  401 N. Washington, Rockville, MD • (800) 638-9636
- **Prodigy**
  445 Hamilton Ave, White Plains, NY • (800) 776-3449

Of these, CompuServe seems to be the leading provider of market-related data, with America On-Line a close runner-up.

The Internet

In addition to membership services that charge you a monthly fee, there is the Internet. Mysterious as it is to some, the Internet is our only avenue of free speech, so far. The Internet is not administered by any single company or governing body; it is true anarchy. As such, the information content is left to the whim (and profitability) of the individual provider.

29

The Internet is the name we give to the pipelines that connect thousands and thousands of computers around the world via modems and phone lines. Each networked computer has a unique address, like 123.456.789.123 that functions rather like a zip code. When one computer wants to find another, it just needs the proper address. Various software vendors make software browsers available that allow you to assign names you can remember to these addresses, and that make it easy to search many, many computers for information. Some of the popular browsers are Netscape (which is fast becoming the de facto standard), Mosaic, WebSurfer and NetCruiser.

Furthermore, most of the commercial on-line services offer a link to the Internet. You simply log on to your on-line service (like America On-Line) and click the Internet button.

The only problem then is that to find information on the Internet you have to know where it is. That can be a catch-22 sometimes. One way to find what you're looking for is to use one of the search engines. Most browsers include a button labeled "search" that will take you directly to a search engine. You type in the word(s) you're looking for and away it goes. Sometimes it will return a very broad search totally unrelated to your quest, sometimes it will get you right where you want to go. For instance, searching for the word "data" isn't going to get you very far.

A natural extension of my magazine (*Traders' Catalog & Resource Guide*) was to put it in electronic form, which I did on the Internet at *The Money Mentor* (http://www.moneymentor.com). One of the buttons on *The Money Mentor*'s menu will take you directly to a list of all the sources of data of which I am aware. We scan the Internet daily looking for new resources and link all trading- and investing-related sites to *The Money Mentor*. (See figure 3.1) It's free. Come take a look.

Some of the Internet sites we have found which supply data are:

Money Mentor Quotes	http://www.moneymentor.com
Quote.com 5 free quotes per day for registered users	http://www.quote.com
PCQuote 20-minute delay; free unlimited quotes.	http://www.pcquote.com

Investor's Edge free	http://www.irnet.com
PAWWS unlimited free quotes	http://www.secapl.com/cgi-bin/qs
InterQuote Stock Services real-time and 15-minute delay	http://www.interquote.com
E*Trade Quote Server	http://www.etrade.com/etrade/html/etqmain.htm
NET Worth free quotes; requires registration	http://networth.galt.com/www/home/start.html
DBC Quote Server 15-minute delay; free	http://www.dbc.com/quote.html

If all this seems rather complicated, it's because it is. That's why I put *The Money Mentor* together, so you can come to one site and click a button to link to all the rest.

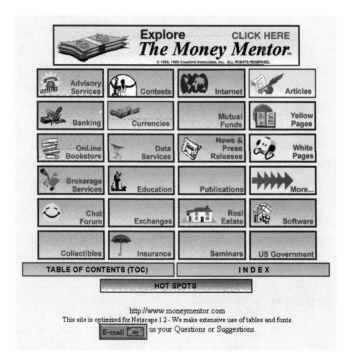

Figure 3.1   The Money Mentor (http://www.moneymentor.com)

4 ANALYZING YOUR DATA

Charting Techniques

While technical analysts tend to believe that all the information you need is in price (and sometimes volume), we don't all agree on how to chart prices.

Essentially we use basic geometry to construct a rectangular diagram of price action. A chart consists of a horizontal and a vertical axis, often called the x- and y-axis respectively, as in Figure 4.1.

To draw your chart, begin with time as the x-axis and price as the y-axis. (More advanced techniques use other values for one or both of these axes, but that's for *Trading 102*.) Estimate the low and potential highs for the instrument you're following, and the time frame you'll be observing. The time frame goes on the x-axis. The price scale goes on the y-axis, as in Figure 4.2. Inevitably, you'll use scotch tape or glue, if you're charting by hand, and extend the x- and y-axes of your chart as shown in Figure 4.3. (That's one of the advantages of using a computer. It automatically scales your charts, and you don't run out of room on your paper.)

Types of Charts

The simplest chart form, **a scatter chart**, shows a dot at each price occurrence, with the x-axis being time, as in Figure 4.4.

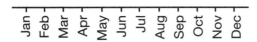

Figure 4.1   X-Axis showing monthly time frame.

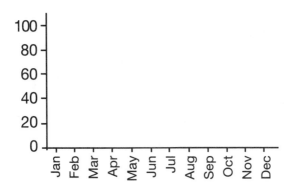

Figure 4.2   The vertical Y-Axis shows price scale.

Figure 4.3   Extended Chart

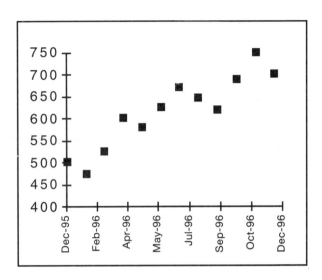

Figure 4.4   A scatter chart.

A **line chart** connects adjacent price dots with a straight line, again with time as the x-axis (See Figure 4.5).

There is some argument about the validity of connecting the price dots with lines, because no trades actually took place anywhere along that line. The value of drawing the line is the visual clarity it gives you. It is easier to see direction and patterns with a line chart than with a scatter chart.

A **bar chart** (See Figure 4.6) uses high, low and closing prices to construct a single bar for each time period.

Each bar represents a single time period, for example, a week, a day, a month, an hour. For that time period, we draw a single vertical line from the highest price to the lowest price experienced during that period (See Figure 4.7).

Then we make a small horizontal mark on the left (the beginning of that time period) showing the price at which that time period opened, and a small horizontal mark on the right representing the price at which that period ended (See Figure 4.8).

For illustration, let's take a look at the Dow Jones Industrial Average. On June 1, 1995, the DJIA opened at 4465.14. On June 30, 1995, the

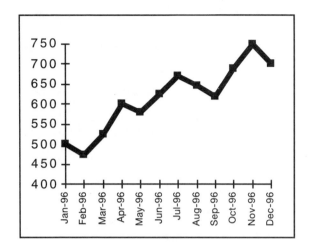

Figure 4.5   A line chart.

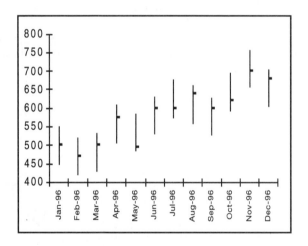

Figure 4.6   A bar chart.

Figure 4.7   A bar showing only high and low.

35

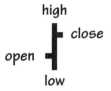

Figure 4.8 A bar showing the open, high, low, and close of the period.

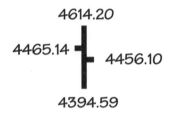

Figure 4.9 A single monthly bar showing open, high, low, and close.

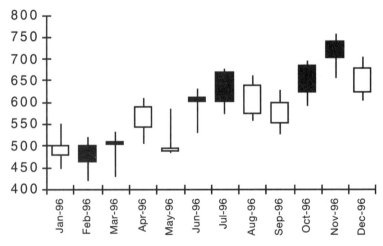

Figure 4.10 Japanese Candlesticks.

DJIA closed at 4456.10. During June of 1995, the highest price the DJIA ever experienced was 4614.20 (on 6/22/95) and the lowest price was 4394.59 (on 6/9/95). That information is presented in Figure 4.9.

A **Japanese Candlestick** chart uses the same information as a bar chart, but with an additional piece of information, direction. Figure 4.10 shows how we construct candlestick charts.

A candlestick is a bar — with width and color. The width of each bar is fixed and represents the range between that session's opening and closing. The color of the bar indicates direction.

Later in this chapter we discuss candlestick charting further.

Another chart type that shows open, high, low and close as well as direction is used by Glenn Neely of The Elliott Wave Institute. Glenn's charts show each "bar" as a small chart in itself. While a traditional bar is shown in Figure 4.11, a NEoWave bar would also show direction (See Figure 4.12).

Point and Figure charting was developed by Charles Dow, after whom we've named the Dow Jones Industrial Average and Dow Theory. Dow's original charts showed prices and their direction without regard to time. While prices were moving up he wrote the whole dollar price values in a single column, each one on top of the previous price. When prices reversed and began moving down, his chart would move over one column and prices were written below one another in a stack. Original point and figure charts looked like the chart in Figure 4.13.

Figure 4.11 A traditional bar.

Figure 4.12 A NEoWave bar.

		47	47
		46	46
45	45	45	45
44	44	44	
43			

Figure 4.13 *Original point and figure charting.*

This concept was later expanded, using Xs for up moves and Os for down moves and accounting for jerky up and down moves, by moving over a column only when price has moved up or down more than a certain amount, called the box size.

Definition:

Box

The area of a point-and-figure chart into which the technician places one X or O, representing a given amount of price increase or decrease represented by a box on a point-and-figure chart

Point and figure charts do not consider time. (See Figure 4.14) A point and figure technician said aptly, "If all the information you need is in price, why do you chart time?"

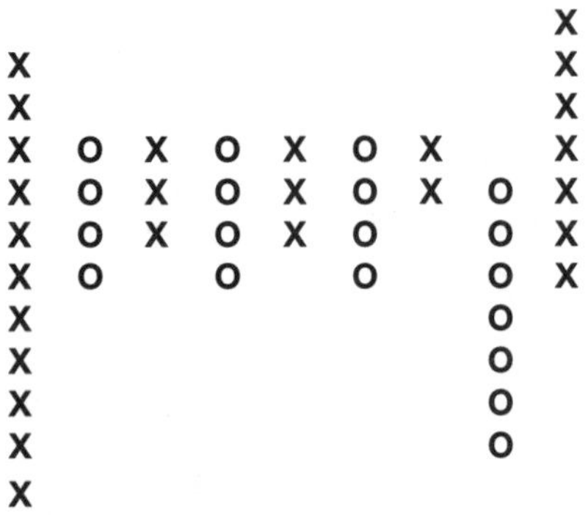

```
                                      X
        X                             X
        X                             X
        X   O   X   O   X   O   X     X
        X   O   X   O   X   O   X   O X
        X   O   X   O   X   O       O X
        X   O       O       O       O X
        X                           O
        X                           O
        X                           O
        X                           O
        X
```

Figure 4.14 A point and figure chart.

The study of point and figure charting includes analytical techniques which are a science in themselves. For in-depth study of this technology, read *Point & Figure Charting* by Thomas J. Dorsey.

Technical Indicators

Most of today's popular technical analysis software comes with a variety of technical indicators preprogrammed for your use. The equations are built-in; you simply load your chart and click on the indicator you want. The software performs the calculations and displays the chart.

Unless you have some understanding of the theory behind the calculations, you'll simply be looking at meaningless squiggles on a computer monitor.

In his book *Technical Analysis from A to Z,* Steven B. Achelis (who is president and founder of Equis, a leading maker of financial software) defines most of the popular indicators, giving an overview, interpretation, and example with each definition. Pick up a copy of "TAZ" at your local bookstore before you start using any of the indicators in any of the software packages.

While it may be elegant to have four forks on the left and three knives and three spoons on the right for a formal meal, one of each will get the job done just as well. As a beginner (or even as a pro) you don't need dozens of indicators. All you really need is one good one! Here are a few of the standard technical indicators and their uses.

Definition:

Average Directional Movement Index (ADX)
A technical indicator developed by J. Welles Wilder, which measures the intensity of a market's trend. An increasing ADX means a trend is in progress; a decreasing ADX means the market is not trending

For a complete explanation of the development and calculation of ADX consult *New Concepts in Technical Trading Systems* by J. Welles Wilder, Jr.

ADX is a very powerful tool, as it reveals trends (see Figure 4.15). It does not tell you the direction of the trend (use a moving average for that), it just tells you that there is a trend.

Markets trend about 30 percent of the time. That means that markets do not trend about 70 percent of the time. Your studies might lead you to become a trend follower, or they might lead you to trade channels in sideways patterns. In either case, you had better know which stage the market is in!

The trick with ADX, as with all technical indicators, is to find just the right parameters to use to create a profitable system. Choosing a small number for the length parameter will show you short-term trends, which a large number will show you long-term trends.

Candlesticks

Candlestick charts, developed by the Japanese, are older than bar charts and point and figure charts, but have only recently come into use in the U.S. Steve Nison is the acknowledged Western expert on candlestick charting techniques, and makes this information available in *Japanese Candlestick Charting Techniques.*

A candlestick is a bar—with width and color, as in Figure 4.16. The width of each bar is fixed and represents the range between that session's opening and closing. This part of the bar is called the body or real body. The color of the bar indicates direction. If the body is filled (usually black), it means the close was lower than the open—a down bar. An up session is indicated by leaving the body empty, or white. The thin lines

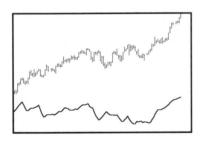 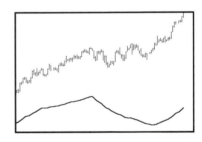

Figure 4.15 ADX showing short-term and long-term trends.

40

above and below the body of the candlestick are called shadows. These lines represent the extremes, the highs and lows, of the bar.

Years of study can be spent just getting the basics of candlestick charting and the implications of its many patterns, called revealing names like "hanging man," "dark cloud cover," and "morning star." If this specialty of technical analysis interests you, start with Nison, then read *The Japanese Chart of Charts* by Seiki Shimizu and expand from there.

While many of the popular software packages offer candlestick charting as an indicator, only specialty packages offer interpretation of the patterns. *The Candlestick Forecaster* by International Pacific Trading Company, *Kabuto Super Power* by Marketsoft & Research, Ltd., and *CandlePower5* by North Systems all offer candlestick interpretation as well as charting. (See the Appendix for specifics on software vendors.)

Cycles

Cyclical analysis stems from the belief that history repeats itself. The ancients knew about cycles; they documented seasons and lunar cycles, and made calendars. In its simplest form, a financial cycle is

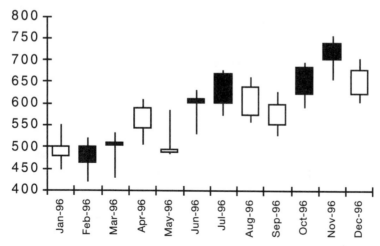

Figure 4.16 Candlestick charting.

measured as the distance between successive lows or successive highs in price behavior. John F. Ehlers (to my mind the undisputed forerunner of computerized cycle analysis for the markets) in *MESA and Trading Market Cycles*, aptly states:

> *The fact that cycles exist does not imply that they exist all the time. Cycles come and go. External events sometimes dominate and obscure existing cycles. Experience shows that cycles useful for trading are present only about 15 to 30 percent of the time.*

Cycles analysis involves the study of overlapping cycles, as well as external influences and quickly evolves into harmonic analysis.

If you become interested in cycles analysis and want to read further, start with *MESA and Trading Market Cycles* by John F. Ehlers, *Cyclic Analysis in Futures Trading* by Jacob Bernstein and *The Spiral Calendar* by Christopher Carolan.

You might also want to contact the Foundation for the Study of Cycles, 900 W. Valley Rd, Ste 502, Wayne, PA 19087, (610) 995-2120.

Elliott

R.N. Elliott, the father of this theory, began formulating his ideas and principles before the crash of 1929, while convalescing from a serious illness. *The Wave Principle* was not published until 1938, and in 1946 he

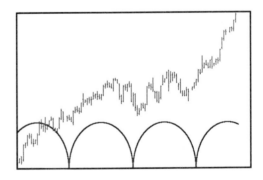

Figure 4.17 Simple cycles equidistant from a significant low.

published *Nature's Law—The Secret of the Universe*. Elliott believed that his theories were part of the law of the universe, which governs all of man's activities.

Closely aligned with the work of 13th century mathematician Leonardo de Pisa, son of Bonaccio (which shortens to Filius Bonacci or FiBonacci), the theory holds that there are repetitive, rhythmical patterns in nature, which in this case form the pattern of five waves up and three waves down, as in Figure 4.18.

In a bear market, the wave count would be upside down, in other words five waves down, and three waves up.

Within each wave is another series of five and three waves, like the wooden dolls one inside of another, going on indefinitely, as in Figure 4.19.

The waves have a definite mathematical relationship to each other, based on ratios of Fibonacci numbers, with the ratios 0.618 and 1.618 being dominant factors.

Figure 4.18 Five waves up and three waves down.

Figure 4.19 Waves within waves.

The trick with Elliott Wave analysis is to properly recognize the wave count. Elliotticians count the waves as in Figure 4.20.

Once again, this is one of those IF ... THEN situations. If you can reliably recognize the 1 wave, or even the 1 and 2 waves, then the theory is predictive—you'll know where the market is headed for the 3, 4, and 5 waves.

Two software products come to mind for Elliott Wave analysis: *Advanced G.E.T.* by Trading Techniques, Inc., and *Elliott Wave Analyser* by the Center for Elliott Wave Analysis.

Figure 4.21 is a screen capture from *Elliott Wave Analyser*, and shows a sample of the program's ability to run through thousands of calculations in order to determine the most likely wave count and label the waves accordingly.

An excellent introduction to Elliott Wave theory is found in John Murphy's *Technical Analysis of the Futures Markets*. Two other books you should study if this theory interests you are: *The Major Works of R.N. Elliott* edited by Robert Prechter and *Elliott Wave Principle* by A.J. Frost and Robert Prechter.

Gann

W.D. Gann was a legendary stock and commodity trader in the first half of the twentieth century. His work is often mysterious and seemingly based on mathematical and geometric principles combined with astrology and biblical references.

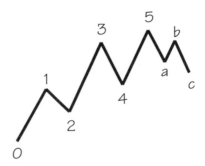

Figure 4.20 Counting the waves.

Gann Analysis makes use of important constant angles like 30°, 45°, 60°, 90° as divisions of the 360° circle, as well as squares of numbers, like 9, 16, 25, etc. Well known in Gann Analysis is the Gann Square or Gann Wheel from which analysts are able to pinpoint support and resistance areas with angles drawn from the origin at the center. This square of numbers is formed by placing the beginning price in the center of the square and incrementing clockwise (See Figure 4.22).

Analysts then watch the prices on the important angles for support and resistance (See Figure 4.23).

Technical analysis software often provides tools for drawing Gann angles and squares. With this form of analysis it is important that the size of the squares match the harmonics of the stock or commodity in question, so don't just grab the tool and think your analysis is done. Figure 4.24 shows Gann angles and squares as drawn by the computer software and Figure 4.25 shows a Gann Wheel.

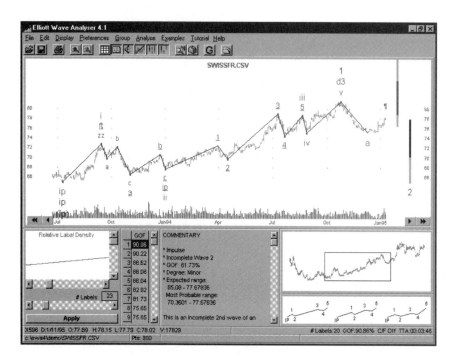

Figure 4.21 Screen capture from Elliott Wave Analyser

This is about as rudimentary as it gets with Gann analysis. It is a very complex field requiring years of study. For a clear and concise introduction to the concepts, see John Murphy's *Technical Analysis of the Futures Markets*. If you are interested in delving further, a subscription to *Traders'*

```
250  255  260  265  270  275  280
245  160  165  170  175  180  285
240  155  110  115  120  185  290
235  150  105  100  125  190  295
230  145  140  135  130  195  300
225  220  215  210  205  200  305
```

Figure 4.22   Gann Square

```
250  255  260  265  270  275  280
245  160  165  170  175  180  285
240  155  110  115  120  185  290
235  150  105  100  125  190  295
230  145  140  135  130  195  300
225  220  215  210  205  200  305
```

Figure 4.23 Gann Square with an important angle marked.

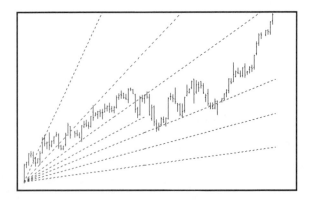

Figure 4.24 Gann Fann generated by software.

World magazine is in order. This quarterly publication explores Gann and Elliott work as well as astrological analysis and is available from Larry Jacobs at Halliker's Inc.

Much of Gann's original and reprinted work is maintained by Nikki Jones of Lambert-Gann Publishing. One of the more fascinating works of Gann is *Tunnel Thru the Air or Looking Back from 1940,* which he wrote in 1927. Many of the events, inventions, market panics and booms mentioned in this book actually came about in later years. In the foreword Gann confidently states: "This story is founded on facts and events ... which will happen in the future."

MACD

Introduced in 1979 by Gerald Appel, MACD stands for Moving Average Convergence Divergence. MACD is the difference between two exponential moving averages, one faster than the other and an exponential average of the difference between the two moving averages. The original

Figure 4.25 Gann Wheel.

20-page pamphlet, *The Moving Average Convergence-Divergence Trading Method—Advanced Version* by Gerald Appel explains his calculations and methodology.

Most popular software sets the default values for the MACD at 12, 26, 9 for the first and second exponential averages and the period of the exponential average of the difference respectively. I have found that experimentation with these numbers is in order and that different markets follow different periodicities. Study the examples of the S&P500 in Figure 4.26, one with the values of the MACD set at the default 12, 26, 9 and the second with the values set much closer together at 9, 13, 7.

The crossover points on the second MACD occur sooner, potentially giving earlier market timing signals.

In *Short-Term Trading in Futures*, Jake Bernstein employs MACD, which he calls DEMA (Dual Exponential Moving Averages) in excellent examples of trading systems. I highly recommend this book as a quick-start for all traders, not just futures traders.

Remember that technical analysis and charting methods are of general application, and don't be frightened just because a book has the word "futures" in the title.

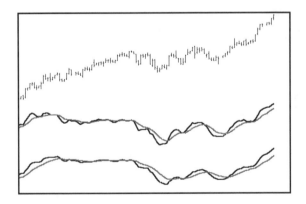

Figure 4.26 MACD 12, 26, 9 and MACD 9, 13, 7.

McClellan Oscillator

The popular McClellan Oscillator is an interpretation of the advance-decline line which was developed by Sherman and Marian McClellan and which measures the short-term overbought/oversold condition of the market as a whole, using the NYSE as proxy (see Figure 4.27).

The companion indicator, the McClellan Summation Index, shows the intermediate to long-term direction of the market—up or down. These two indicators are relatively straightforward and a great place to start your analysis and research.

The formulas for the oscillator and the summation index are in the Glossary.

For further reading, the definitive work on these indicators is by the McClellans themselves in *Patterns for Profit*. Another source for how-to, as well as current interpretation of the McClellans' work is the debonair Mr. Kennedy Gammage of The Richland Company. Ken authored *The Special Orientation Report* which does an admirable job of summarizing the construction and use of the oscillator and summation index.

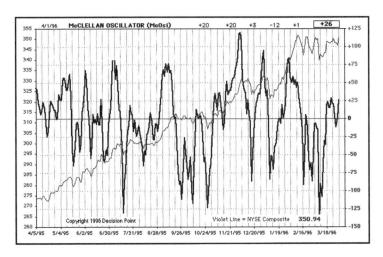

Figure 4.27 McClellan Oscillator. Chart provided by Carl Swenlin, Decision Point.

Momentum

Webster defines momentum as "the impetus of a moving object." That definition gives me a better mental picture of its use in the markets than the standard used by technical analysts.

Definition:

Momentum

Velocity of price change over the momentum period.

$$M = C_0 - C_i$$

where C_0 is the current closing price and C_i is the closing price i time periods ago.

Steven Achelis in *Technical Analysis from A to Z* defines momentum as a measure of "the amount that a security's price has changed over a given time span."

Observation of momentum will tell you the speed of the market. I look at momentum as a measure of rate-of-change, which tells me how many dollars per hour a security moves. There is only one reason to trade: to make money. Given that as your premise, you better know how much money potential there is in a given instrument. Interpretation of momentum is where you find that answer.

Moving Averages

A moving average is a way to smooth the noise in data so that the trend is easier to see. (See Figure 4.28)

Mathematically a simple moving average is the sum of a value plus a selected number of previous values divided by the total number of values.

$$MAV = [V_1 + V_2 + ... + V_n] / n$$

Moving averages can be simple, weighted or exponential. The equation above calculates a simple moving average, the total of values divided by the number of values. This type of averaging gives equal weight to each day's values.

What if the characteristics of the market are changing, so that the data closer to now is more important than the data a long time ago? A weighted moving average gives more importance to the more recent values by use of multipliers (weighting factors). (See Figure 4.29) The furthest value is multiplied by one, the second value by two, and so on until coming to the most recent data. For instance, with 5 data values, the first is multiplied by 1, the second by 2, the third by 3, the fourth by 4 and the fifth by 5. Then the sum of all these products is divided by the sum of the multipliers $(1 + 2 + 3 + 4 + 5 = 15$ in this case).

$$WMAV = \frac{\{ [n-(n-1)]*V_1 + [n-(n-2)]*V_2 + ... + n*V_n \}}{\{ n + (n-1) + (n-2) + ... + [n-(n-1)] \}}$$

The weighted moving average weights the recent data more heavily than older data. Still, both this and the simple moving average only take into account the data in the specific time frame, or window of time.

To take into account all the known data for a security or contract, we would use an exponential moving average (emav), which begins with the first value and accumulates the data while it gives more weight to the more recent data. This is not a calculation you'll want to run by hand, so don't plan on using exponential moving averages without a computer.

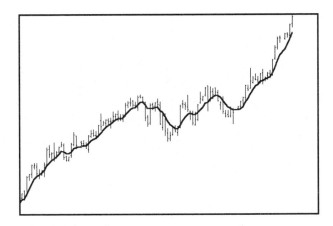

Figure 4.28 Simple Moving Average.

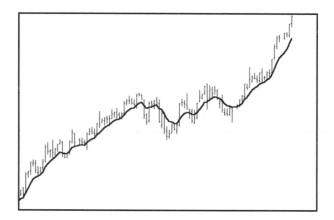

Figure 4.29 Weighted Moving Average.

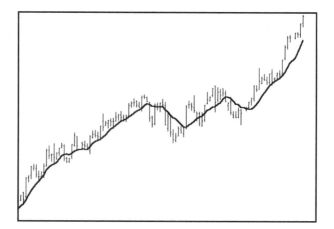

Figure 4.30 Exponential Moving Average.

For my trading, I use exponential moving averages which I have "tweaked" mathematically, but they're still moving averages.

EMAVs seem to give more timely signals, especially in faster markets.

$$A_i = \alpha P_i + (1-\alpha)A_{i-1}$$

where P is the price on day i and a (alpha) is a smoothing constant ($0<a<1$). Alpha may be estimated as $2/(n+1)$, where n is the simple moving average length.

Most of the popular technical analysis software products have all three of these moving average types available as indicators, so you don't have to calculate anything, you just click on the chart and click on the indicator you want.

Pattern Recognition

Pattern recognition is a matter of repeatedly asking the question "What is true here?" Probably the most prolific pattern recognizer in this business is Larry Williams, whose books *The Definitive Guide to Futures Trading* and *The Definitive Guide to Futures Trading Volume II* can give you a good foundation in the process of recognizing patterns.

Larry is an ace at recognizing patterns in the market and then applying statistical analysis to get an idea of how often this pattern occurs and the likelihood of making a winning trade when you see the pattern again.

Pattern recognition is kind of like one of those kid's word puzzles, where you are to circle all the words you see:

```
A  V  C  Y  C  L  E
Q  O  Z  U  A  O  A
B  L  A  C  K  X  R
M  U  D  P  I  E  T
X  M  Y  W  A  N  H
E  E  L  M  A  V  S
```

Rather than trying to decipher a jumble of letters, you're analyzing a jumble of numbers or visually inspecting patterns in charts.

For instance, in *The Definitive Guide to Futures Trading Volume II*, Larry Williams notes that:

> *If we have 3 consecutive down closes in the S&P, you have a 64.6 percent probability of an up day tomorrow.*

The pattern is three consecutive down closes followed by an up day. The statistical analysis tells you how likely the pattern is to happen.

Computer Software

There are hundreds of software products that will produce charts for traders. The obvious advantage to using software is speed. The drawback to using software, especially in the beginning of your training, is that you don't get a "feel" for the market you are studying like you do when you create all your charts by hand.

When racing sports cars, one first looks at the track, then walks the track several times, then drives the track slowly before considering actually driving the track with any speed. Walking the track allows your body's memory to incorporate distance and curves into its neurology.

If you begin your trading career by making all your charts by hand, your neurology will suggest theories for trading systems later on when you do your research. Something happens in your subconscious when you draw one bar at a time over a long time frame, which reveals itself later as "intuition."

Therefore, even if all your trading and research is going to be computerized, start by making your charts with pencil and paper. After your subconscious is atuned to the market you can begin to work with computerized charts. If you begin with computer generated charts you'll find that you miss the nuances of the market and can't quite ever seem to find a system that really works.

As in televised cooking shows where they mix up the batter and then take a finished cake out of the oven, let's skip to the point in time where you are intimately familiar with the markets you have been studying. That could be several months or several years. By that time you will know what type of charting interests you, and can intelligently select software to perform the charting function.

What software will not do is generate ideas. You must hold brainstorming sessions. Customarily brainstorming sessions are conducted in a room with a white-board and markers, a person who acts not as moderator but as clerk to write down the ideas, and all the people involved in a project. A question is brought under consideration and everyone speaks freely as ideas come to mind.

As a trader you will have brainstorming sessions with yourself. Write down all possible research avenues as they occur to you. I always keep a small six-ring binder with me in which to write these notes. You never know when these ideas will pop to the surface.

The Analysis Process

What's the goal here? Without a specific goal, you are not going to achieve one.

Goals like "I wanna be rich" are not specific. This is not an easy field in which to become rich. In fact, this is not an easy field in which to even make a living. The easy part is to lose all your trading capital and give up.

In the analysis process you are going to look at thousands of charts and ask yourself the question "What is true here?" We're working a complicated logic problem. Here's where your brainstorming comes in. Let's look at the chart in Figure 4.31 and brainstorm together.

Now, let's begin to ask "What is true here?" It is true that the market (it doesn't matter what market this is) moves sharply upward in the beginning, then moves sideways for most of the chart, and towards the end moves sharply upward again. It is true that there are several smaller

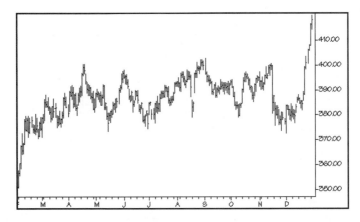

Figure 4.31 Brainstorm with this chart.

moves within the large moves. It is true that some of the bars in this chart appear volatile, that is the range (the distance between the high and low) appears large compared to some of the other bars in this chart.

Before applying any indicators or trend lines to this chart, I always ask whether it is worth my time. This is your job and you need to be paid a decent hourly wage. What hourly wage will this market allow? How do you figure that out?

First, let's mark the obvious highs and lows on the chart (Figure 4.32). We'll use up-triangles to denote a low (from which the market moves up) and a down-triangle to denote a high (from which the market moves down).

We don't know yet whether there's any money to be made here, we've just marked potential entry points and exit points.

Next we need to look at the scale of this chart to see whether the market movements between our entries and exits would be profitable. If, for instance, the time frame of this chart were a year and each move would only give us a couple of dollars profit, it's not worth our time. But, if it's a year and each move produces thousand of dollars, we'll go further with our analysis.

The scale on the right side of the chart shows that the data moves from 350 to 410, a 60 point move. This chart happens to be of the S&P

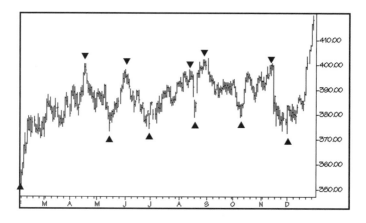

Figure 4.32 Mark potential entries and exits.

500 (my favorite trading vehicle), but it doesn't matter what we're observing, the test for fitness is the same. In the S&P 500, a move of one point is worth $500, so a move from 350 to 410 would be worth 60 * $500, or $30,000. The time frame in question is from February through December, a period of eleven months. Thirty thousand dollars in eleven months, that's $2,727 per month, or $16 per hour. That's our first rough approximation, but the answer is yes, this looks to be tradable.

Next we'll pretend that we could correctly catch each trade we've marked at the precise highs and lows. We'll calculate each trade's profit or loss and see what hourly wage could have been produced. The trades are displayed in Figure 4.33.

This type of trading system is called a **reversal system**, because each trade closes one position and opens another. You are always in the market, either long or short. Note that we have used closing prices for all the trades. The assumption here is that we have bought or sold the market at the closing price of the day, not any of the intra-day prices.

Calculating our potential hourly wage, we find that $147,500 in 11 months is $13,400 per month, or $80 per hour. That's respectable.

trade nbr	type	date	entry	date	exit	profit/loss
1	buy	1-Feb	350	25-Apr	400	$25,000
2	sell	25-Apr	400	10-May	375	$12,500
3	buy	10-May	375	1-Jun	400	$12,500
4	sell	1-Jun	400	1-Jul	375	$12,500
5	buy	1-Jul	375	12-Aug	400	$12,500
6	sell	12-Aug	400	16-Aug	380	$10,000
7	buy	16-Aug	380	1-Sep	400	$10,000
8	sell	1-Sep	400	10-Oct	380	$10,000
9	buy	10-Oct	380	4-Nov	400	$10,000
10	sell	4-Nov	400	1-Dec	375	$12,500
11	buy	1-Dec	375	31-Dec	415	$20,000
					TOTAL	$147,500

Figure 4.33 Trading log of potential entries and exits.

Now for a moment of truth. Before we can go any further we must take a second look at our pretense of catching each market move at the top and the bottom. That'll never happen. As a rule of thumb, I make the assumption that a good system can catch 60 percent of each market move. That's pretty realistic. With this in mind, 60 percent of $147,500 is $88,500, which is $48.27 per hour. Still respectable. Using 2,000 hours per year as a quick estimate, that gives us $96,545 per year trading one contract.

I call this part of the data analysis the "potential hourly wage analysis," or PHW. Before jumping into the numerical or pattern analysis phase, it's important to conduct these calculations. If the hourly wage is not acceptable, why would you want to spend time conducting all the remaining research?

Digital vs. Analog Analysis

In the early days of computer technology there was great debate about whether the digital or the analog computer would win over the marketplace. Likewise, there is debate among technical analysts about whether the answers to the market's movement lies in digital or analog analysis.

What's the difference? Digital analysis is discrete, that is, each point of analysis is separate and distinct from the next. Digital analysis looks like a scatter chart (Figure 4.34).

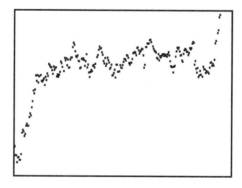

Figure 4.34 Discrete points; digital analysis.

On the other hand, analog analysis is continuous, whether or not the data is. Analog analysis looks like an average of the connected points (Figure 4.35). Analog analysis interpolates between points, creating data where there is none. Digital analysis assumes that patterns repeat themselves.

Numerical Analysis

Numerical analysis is the process of finding equations that describe the movement we observe in the market.

Numerical analysis can be as simple as drawing a straight line showing the market's direction. That's called a **trend line**. Or, it can be as complex as multiple sets of non-linear equations or neural networks. Most of the technical indicators described earlier in this chapter are numerical in nature. Further, most technical indicators are numerical in nature.

How do we use numerical analysis? Let's look back to the chart with the up and down arrows. That chart exhibits the ideal system: it catches all the highs and lows. Our goal, then, is to get as close to this as we can with equations. We'll begin our search with moving averages. In Chapter 15 we'll go into the process in depth.

With technical analysis software (MetaStock, TradeStation, SuperCharts, TickerWatcher, SMARTrader, Windows on Wallstreet, etc.) I overlay an eighteen-period moving average on the chart (Figure 4.36)

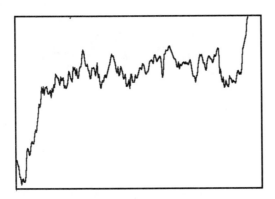

Figure 4.35 *Connected points; analog analysis.*

On inspection I see that this moving average is too slow. It does not turn as fast as the market turns. After some experimentation with input values, we find that a five-period moving average looks pretty good (Figure 4.37).

Numerical analysis can take this form, where we use a prepackaged computer program to overlay indicators and test ideas, or it can become as complicated as writing your own programs to analyze the raw data. That process is well beyond the scope of this book, however, and is left for *Trading 103*.

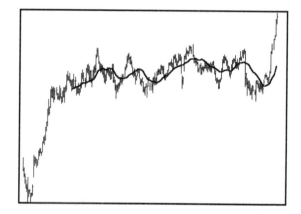

Figure 4.36 Eighteen period moving average.

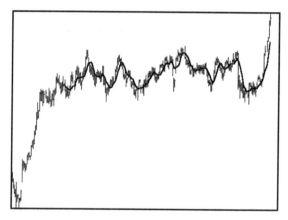

Figure 4.37 Five period moving average.

Pattern Analysis

Pattern recognition is the process of finding recurring patterns in the market movement we observe.

Pattern recognition is a matter of repeatedly asking the question "What is true here?" Probably the most prolific pattern recognizer in this business is Larry Williams, whose books *The Definitive Guide to Futures Trading* and *The Definitive Guide to Futures Trading Volume II* can give you a good foundation in the process of recognizing patterns.

Larry is an ace at recognizing patterns in the market and then applying statistical analysis to get an idea of how often this pattern occurs and the likelihood of making a winning trade when you see the pattern again.

Here, for instance, is an example of a pattern Larry revealed at a recent meeting of technical analysts:

> *The pattern is setup when there is a day whose low is the lowest low of the last 4 days and has a down close. If the close two days after this low range day is greater than the low day's high, buy on the close.*

A pictorial representation of the pattern is shown in Figure 4.38.

Figure 4.38 A typical Larry Williams pattern setup.

Pattern analysis is in many ways more difficult than numerical analysis, because you can't just throw a computer program on it and crunch away. Look at the intricacies of it. The pattern in Figure 4.38 is a small section of a much larger chart. Would you have seen that pattern in a forest full of bars? If this type of analysis interests you, Larry Williams can be reached at CTI Publishing, 1-800-800-8333.

5 EXPLORING THE LITERATURE

Hundreds of books have been written about financial matters, with topics ranging from *Advanced Commodity Trading Techniques* to *Zen in the Markets*. It's difficult to read them all, so let's first look at a few which I believe are on the "required reading" list for new traders.

Be Your Own Financial Planner—Total Money Management in 21 Days (by Dorlene V. Shane)

Loaded with examples and worksheets, this self-study guide walks you through your entire financial picture, helping you get organized. It's amazing how many traders don't have their personal lives in order.

While this exercise is more about your personal finances than about your trading portfolio, once you've completed this book you will have a much better idea how much capital you have to risk trading. Further, the process you experience is one you can mimic in your trading money management techniques.

Contrary Investing—The Insider's Guide to Buying Low and Selling High (by Richard E. Band)

Richard Band, Editor of Personal Finance, publishes one of the nation's most widely read investment newsletters. His market forecasts have been quoted in Business Week, USA Today, and other national publications, and he has appeared on CBS News and the Public Broadcasting Service.

In this book Band presents simple, sane, and reliable techniques for contrary investing. He lists signs of impending market reversals, a stock trading system, a contrarian approach to investing in mutual funds, and ways to spot tops and bottoms in the real estate market.

Economics—A Self-Teaching Guide (by Stephen L. Slavin)

A sound foundation in the theory of economics will stead you well in your preparation for trading. Understanding what others think moves the economy will give you a foundation from which you can begin to question the standard principles and begin to form your own.

Economics: A Self-Teaching Guide is probably the easiest to handle and yet most thorough guide you can find to lead you through this process. Beginning with a short history lesson and moving right into a review of the mathematics and charting techniques you will need, this book covers supply and demand, Gross National Product, consumption, inflation, unemployment, fiscal policy, and the Federal Reserve in a way that makes it all seem easy.

At the end of each chapter is a short test, with answers, to help you review the preceding material. This step-by-step, self-paced format makes the learning process fun.

According to the jacket cover, "Steven Slavin is Associate Professor of Economics at Union County College in Cranford, NJ. He has also taught at Brooklyn College and at the New York Institute of Technology."

A Short History of Financial Euphoria (by John Kenneth Galbraith)

John Kenneth Galbraith is Professor of Economics Emeritus at Harvard University and was the U.S. Ambassador to India during the Kennedy administration. His works include *The Great Crash 1929, The*

Affluent Society, *The New Industrial State*, and *Economics and the Public Purpose*.

A mere 113 page pocket book, *A Short History of Financial Euphoria* will do more to enlighten you about the nature of the markets than any other book of which I am aware. Entertaining and educational, this book will show you why the market not only has, but will continue to have periods of boom and bust.

The Intelligent Investor (by Benjamin Graham)

Former president of the Graham-Newman Corporation and Columbia University Graduate School of Business teacher, Benjamin Graham provides a conservative and safe approach to investing, making a strong case of stock investment strategies.

Keys to Understanding the Financial News

One of the Barron's Business Keys series, this little pocket book is packed with quick-reference explanations of Leading Economic Indicators, the Federal Reserve system, money supply, interest rates, productivity, stock, over-the-counter market, mutual funds, advisory services, municipal bonds, futures, corporate information, and mergers and acquisitions.

By Nick Apostolou and D. Lawrence Cumbley, *Keys to Understanding the Financial News* gives you a short-cut to mastering key concepts and financial terminology.

Money Guide: The Stock Market

The editors of *Money* magazine have put together a clear, concise guide with strategies and tactics for surviving on Wall Street. I don't buy their claim that it can "... be the avenue to Easy Street," but I do believe they do a good job of summarizing the process.

Covering initial public offerings, over-the-counter stocks, Value Line, Standard and Poors, annual reports, takeovers and turnarounds, options, foreign stocks, and margin accounts, this little book will give you a good foundation in the essentials of stock trading.

Options as a Strategic Investment—A Comprehensive Analysis of Listed Option Strategies (by Lawrence G. McMillan)

This one's a toughie. Even though it is difficult reading, it's the book to read on options. Formatted like a college math or physics text, this encyclopedia of options trading is a full semester's work. Every equation, all the explanation and all the examples you could ever ask for will give you the complete course on trading options.

Strategic Investment Timing (by Dick A. Stoken)

Unassuming in appearance, *Strategic Investment Timing* is loaded with information. If you've ever wondered if there is a right time to invest in real estate and a right time to invest in bonds and another right time for stocks, this book will answer all your questions.

With historical examples and statistics, Dick builds his case for market timing. He tells you where to easily find the numbers you'll need to track market activity and measure the investment climate. You'll even learn how to predict presidential elections and what to invest in during both inflationary and deflationary times.

Technical Analysis of the Futures Markets: A Comprehensive Guide to Trading Methods and Applications (by John J. Murphy)

This is the one book which I would say you must memorize. I did. Of the many books on technical analysis, this one is at the same time the most comprehensive and the easiest to understand. John hosts a financial show on CNBC called *Tech Talk*, where you can see him in action, addressing current market issues and answering technical questions. This book doesn't just give you a list of indicators and their equations, it gives you all the explanation and examples you need to understand them. I have two copies of this book, one of which is completely worn out.

Technical Analysis from A to Z (by Steven B. Achelis)

President and founder of Equis International, a leading maker of financial software, Steven Achelis has provided a clear and concise guide to technical indicators. One hundred indicators are explored, giving an overview, interpretation, and example of each. Where applicable, equations and calculation methods are given.

The Ultimate Mutual Fund Guide (by Warren Boroson)

Mutual fund timing and switching is perhaps the best initial entry to trading. It's certainly less risky than options or futures, and you can begin your education with a relatively small outlay of capital.

If you're considering this approach, you need a solid foundation in the overall theory of mutual funds. *The Ultimate Mutual Fund Guide* is the synthesis of the author's poll of seventeen mutual fund authorities, giving you a comprehensive analysis of the expert's choices for best funds.

Wall Street Journal Guide to Understanding Money & Markets

Shaped rather like a travel guide, this 120 page book consists of pictures with explanations. It covers the basics of stocks, bonds, mutual funds, futures, options, and money. If you're just starting out (isn't that what the "101" in the title stands for?) the *Wall Street Journal Guide* ... will give you all the answers to those questions you're embarrassed to ask the professionals. Don't forget, I spent the first month asking "what's a put and what's a call?"

Upward and Onward

The books listed above constitute your beginning study list. Once you completely understand each of the above books you can move on to books that explore these topics in greater detail, and you can begin to study some of the fun stuff. The fun stuff includes proclamations of outrageous success, books which purport to reveal trading systems, and tales of inside, true-life experience.

Don't start with the fun stuff. If you do, you'll get the mistaken impression that trading is loads of excitement, easy riches, and being in the right place at the right time. It's not. Trading is a lot of hard work, study, and research, followed by a lot of hard work, concentration, and discipline.

An extended book list is provided in the Appendix, alphabetical by author. This list doesn't tell you what to read next, but it will give you an idea of the volume of material that is available to you. Probably the best idea at this point is for you to contact several of the mail-order booksellers and request their catalog. From that you can read about each book and decide where to aim your specialized study.

- Lambert-Gann Publishing   1-509-843-1094
- Fraser Publishing   1-802-658-0322
- Institute for Options Research   1-800-334-0854
- International Publishing   1-800-488-4149
- Irwin Professional Publishing   1-800-776-2871
- John Wiley & Sons   1-800-879-4539
- Traders' Library   1-800-272-2855
- Traders Press   1-800-927-8222
- Wall Street Books   1-310-476-6732

6 CLUBS & PROFESSIONAL ORGANIZATIONS

Networking

There is a synergy between people working in groups that sparks creativity. For this reason it's a good idea to find a group or groups in your area which are interested in trading and investing. Often local computer users groups will have financial sub-interest groups. And frequently groups which have the word "investing" in their title are more interested in speculating and trading.

The American Association of Individual Investors (AAII), a nonprofit educational organization, holds regular meetings in most cities. Many of the investing software vendors have established users' groups, also meeting regularly. Find a group in your area, and attend meetings during your learning phase. Through this endeavor, you will also connect with other groups and glean ideas you would otherwise not find.

The Market Technician's Association, with headquarters in New York, has local chapters in many of the larger cities. Often these chapters hold monthly or quarterly meetings to which the public is welcome.

Most of the software vendors have users' groups that meet locally. Among those offering regular meetings are the Fast Track Users Group, MetaStock Users Group, and SuperCharts Users Group. In the Appendix you'll find numbers for software vendors; they'll be happy to hear from you.

Don't Get Stuck

While networking and sharing ideas is important in the beginning phases of trading and investing, for some it becomes not the means but the end in itself. Don't confuse attending meetings with trading. At some point, you must develop your own theories, test them, and begin to trade.

Guide to Meetings

We can't possibly provide you with a complete list of all the various meetings, clubs, and other organizations in this book. We try to keep our Internet site, *The Money Mentor*™, up-to-date with times, places, and topics for upcoming meetings. You may look to *The Money Mentor*™ for these particulars, or if you have information to share, we'll put it on the Internet at *The Money Mentor*™ for free. (http://www.moneymentor.com)

Educational and Networking Meetings

Anaheim, CA	Technical Analysts of Southern California
Atlanta	AAII • Third Tuesday of each month at 7:30 p.m. and on the following Saturday at 10:00 a.m. at the New Christian Church, 4961 Buford Hwy. in Chamblee. (affiliated with the Atlanta PC users group.)
Atlanta	FastTrack • Mr. Goswami 1-404-963-7843
Austin	AAII • Second Wednesday of each month 6:00 p.m. at Texas Guaranteed Student Loan Corp. Contact Archie McNeill at 1-512-458-3466.
Boca Raton	AAII • First Wednesday of each month at Boca Teeca Guest House, 5800 N.W. 2nd Av., 2nd floor front, North building. (Affiliated with the PCUG.)
Boston	AAII • Fourth Thursday of each month at the New World Bank, Route 28, South Yarmouth. Call John Englehard II at 1-508-428-8295 for details.

Buffalo	AAII • First Wednesday of each month, 7:00 p.m. in the IBIMUG Education Center, 1333 Strad Ave., Suite 18, North Tonawanda.
Chicago	American Assoc of Individual Investors (AAII) 1-312-280-0170
Cleveland	AAII • Third Wednesday of each month at 7:00 pm. Call Bob Watson for location.
Columbus, IN	FastTrack • Willard Henderson 1-812-376-7766
Columbus, OH	AAII • Third Tuesday of every month at 7:00 p.m. at Northland Terrace, Inc., located at 5700 Karl Rd.
Connecticut	AAII • Third Tuesday of each month at 6:30 p.m. at the Meriden Public Library.
Dallas/Ft. Worth	AAII • Second Monday of each month at 6:30pm at the Preston Royal Library, one block west of the tollway on Royal Lane.
Detroit	AAII • Fourth Saturday of each month at 10:00 a.m. at the Huntington Bank, located south of Maple on the east side of Orchard Lake Rd. in West Bloomfield. Contact Tom Kerley at 1-313-356-5504.
Ft. Lauderdale	Investors Alliance 1-305-491-5100
Hawaii	AAII • Meetings are held monthly. The SIG is supported by a BBS called the Wall Street Connection. The BBS number is 1-808-521-4356.
Houston	AAII • First Wednesday of each month at the HAL-PC Center, 1200 Post Oak Rd. Call C.J. LeLeux at 1-713-771-4728.
Los Angeles	AAII • First Saturday of every even month at 10:30 a.m. at the Fairview Branch Library, 21st Street and Ocean Park Blvd. in Santa Monica.
Los Angeles	(Culver City) MASC - Market Analysts of Southern California. Ramada Inn, 6333 Bristol Pkwy, Culver City, CA. Usually at 2:30 - 4:00 p.m. on the 2nd Wednesday of the month. Frequently rescheduled based on speaker's schedule. Call Brian Carruthers (714) 372-4954.

Los Angeles	N. Hollywood Investors Club • First Wed. of each month at 6:00pm at the Wild Side Theatre, 10945 Camarillo, N. Hollywood, CA 91602. 1-818-506-8838.
Los Angeles	West Coast Cycles Club. Contact Rich Walker at 1-714-502-2273.
Milwaukee	AAII • Meetings are held at 6:30 p.m. prior to AAII chapter meetings.
Mineola, NY	Society of Quantitative Analysts
Minneapolis/St. Paul • AAII • First Thursday of each month at 7:00pm at the Edina Community Center, Rm. 208, 5701 Normandale Dr. Contact Bob Erickson at 1-612-835-3676.
Nashville	AAII • Third Monday of each month at 6:30 p.m. at Clement Auditorium, as part of the Nashville Users Group. Contact Jim Beres at 1-615-646-2634 for information.
New Caanan, CT IBM PC Users Group
New York	Market Technicians Association 1-212-344-1266
New York	New York PC Users Group 1-212-533-6972
New York	Society for the Management of Artificial Intelligence Resources
Park Ridge, NJ	Technical Analysis Study Group
Philadelphia	Association of Mutual Fund Investors (AMFI) 1-215-946-3170
Phoenix	AAII • First Saturday of each month at 9:00am at the Pyle Center, 655 E. Southern Ave., in Tempe.
Pittsburgh	AAII • This group meets at 6:30 p.m. before AAII chapter meetings.
Pittsburgh	FastTrack • Bob Breitenstein 1-412-921-2478
Portland	FastTrack • Jack Alwen 1-503-694-2100
Rockville, MD	FastTrack • Gregg Miller 1-703-860-4876
Rockville, MD	Capital PC User Group 1-301-762-6775

Royal Oak, MI	National Assoc of Investors Corp (NAIC)
Sacramento	AAII • Third Tuesday of each month at 7:30 p.m. at the SMUD Training Bldg., Training Room B, 1708 59th Street.
San Diego	AAII • Computer Aided Investor Group • Second Tuesday of each month at 7:00 p.m. at the public library branch located at 4155 Governor Dr. in the University City area. Dennis Costarakis 1-619-792-4699.
San Francisco	FastTrack • Joe Lavigne - 415-435-5245; Golden Gate FastTrack Users Group. $5 for nonmembers.
San Francisco	Technical Securities Analysts Assoc of San Francisco 1-415-957-1202
Seattle	AAII • Fourth Monday of each month at 7:30 p.m. at the Slater Park Condo Recreation Room, Slater Ave. & N.E. 119th in Kirkland.
Sydney	Australian Technical Analysis Assoc 61-2-545-2605
Tucson, AZ	FastTrack • Brad Becker 1-602-881-7999
Washington, DC	• Society of Market Technicians
Westchester County, NY	• AAII • Third Thursday of each month at the Hackley School in Tarrytown.

Users' Groups

Most of the major software vendors sponsor Users' Groups, which are local groups of people who meet at a certain time and place to compare experiences with that software and share techniques and views on the market. Not only valuable for current users of the software, these meetings are a great way to meet people who can tell you about their satisfaction (or lack thereof) with the software product, and with whom you share a common interest—trading. Call the contact person for information about upcoming meetings, often the times and places vary depending on holidays and speaker availability.

AIQ 1-800-332-2999

Contact Mitch Lagarza at AIQ for Users' Groups in your vicinity.

Equis: MetaStock 1-800-882-3040

Contact Equis directly for a Users Group in your vicinity.

Investors FastTrack 1-504-737-4808

AZ	Phoenix	Tom Neis	1-602-934-1145
AZ	Prescott	Dean Bailey	1-520-776-4383
AZ	Scottsdale	Roger Haxby	1-602-661-0800
AZ	Sun City West	Charles South	1-602-546-6103
AZ	Tucson	Brad Becker	1-602-881-7999
CA	Banning	Lee Akin	1-909-845-5822
CA	Bewlvedere	Joe Lavigne	1-415-435-5245
CA	Los Angeles	Don Gimpel	1-818-591-0160
CA	San Diego	Jim Quinlan	1-619-487-3346
CA	San Jose	Donald Ryan	1-408-263-3718
CA	Tustin	Gordon E. Suiter	1-714-838-3329
CT	West Haven	Milton Spitzbard	1-203-933-2273
DC	Washington	John Matthews	1-301-589-7612
FL	Boca Raton	Robert Lewison	1-407-750-9529
FL	Daytona Beach	Richard Ottaviani	1-904-673-3290
FL	Boynton Beach	Jack Levitt	1-904-677-5191
FL	Ft. Myers	Dick Thomas	1-813-466-6184
FL	Sarasota	Ron Sheff	1-813-365-4711
FL	Tampa	Roland Schnabel	1-813-988-7046
GA	Lawrenceville	K.B.Goswami	1-404-963-7843
IN	Columbus	Willard Henderson	1-812-376-7766
IN	Crown Point	James Adams	1-219-662-7496
LA	Lafayette	Dexter Lyons	1-318-981-9139
KS	Overland Park	Jon Gjovig	1-913-888-9192
MA	Boston	Richard Boroff	1-508-468-3162
MD	Rockville	Jim Rich	1-703-821-7220
MI	Detroit	Jerome Kornheiser	1-313-582-6272
MO	St. Charles	Robert Silverman	1-314-724-8204
NM	Albuquerque	Jim Hetherington	1-505-875-3471
NC	Charlotte	Bill Davis	1-704-896-1237
OK	Ponca City	Marvin Peterson	1-405-762-3265
OH	Cleveland	Ian Abbott	1-216-934-1617
OH	North Olmsted	Gary Harloff	1-216-734-7271
OR	Portland	Jack Alwen	1-503-694-2100
PA	Langhorne	Aaron Coleman	1-215-946-3170

PA	Pittsburgh	Ed Christianson	1-412-371-0368
PA	Pittsburgh	Bob Breitenstein	1-412-921-2478
TX	Austin	Wayne Kroutil	1-512-836-9541
TX	Houston	Ray Schutter	1-713-665-4767
TX	Houston	Tucker Coughlen	1-713-424-3391
TX	Longview	Scott Smith	1-903-759-8712
TX	San Antonio	Joe Bernstein	1-210-492-6601
VT	Quechee	Jack Levitt	1-802-296-7506
WA	Seattle	Ralph Osterman	1-206-649-8419
WI	Racine	Jerome Trandel	1-414-554-1102

Linn Software, Inc. 1-800-546-6842

Linn Software provides an in-house BBS as their electronic users group. If you have their Macintosh software, TickerWatcher, you'll want to trade notes, macros and just chat with kindred spirits online.

Omega Research 1-800-556-2022

Contact Omega Research directly for Users' Groups in your area.

7 EVALUATING SEMINARS & CONFERENCES

To me a seminar, conference, or workshop is worth the fee for attendance if I get one solid idea from it that improves my trading.

If you are looking for boondoggle seminars where you can write-off your playtime, you're in the wrong business and have come to the wrong source. Don't get me wrong, I like my playtime, too. But not at the expense of my trading.

As in any profession, once you get on one mailing list you'll be on them all. When that happens you'll begin to receive mailings about every conceivable get-rich-quick scheme, as well as every work-your-tail-off-and-learn-something seminar and conference. You can't go to them all. It's your job to sort through them to find the ones which will benefit you most.

If you have the time and the money, I suggest you start by going to one of the get-rich-quick seminars. You'll see what they're all about and hopefully get it over with. We are all tempted to believe that someone else has the answer and that this process is easier than we are finding it to be. The lure of instant riches is seductive.

Once you get that out of your system, it's time to start going to serious seminars that will feed you as much information as you can handle. You need to be learning as much as you possibly can.

Many of the software vendors offer relatively inexpensive seminars designed to teach you about their software, in specific, and about trading techniques, in general. OptionVue Systems International (800) 733-6610,

Omega Research (800) 556-2022, and Equis International (800) 882-3040 all offer educational seminars. Call them to ask for a schedule of upcoming seminars.

Futures magazine (from Oster Communications) has two educational branches that sponsor seminars: Futures Learning Center (800) 635-3936 and Futures International Conferences. These seminars are independent of any particular software vendor, and are general in nature, bringing you the latest speakers and their techniques. Oster Communications can be reached at (319) 277-6341.

By far the best seminar for beginning traders, the Telerate Seminars by Tim Slater (formerly called the CompuTrac Seminars), are conducted worldwide. These seminars are not sponsored by a software vendor, but are independently sponsored by Telerate. In the U.S. the seminar is usually held in the fall. While this is not meant to be an advertisement for their sessions, they do a fantastic job of enlisting speakers from the trading community who are leading-edge in their fields. The speakers are not employed by Telerate Seminars, but are brought in just for these talks which take place over three days. Each year the seminar brings new speakers, making it wise to attend year after year to stay on top of the latest in techniques and technologies. The 3 days of learning are intense and challenging as well as fun. Tim Slater can be reached at (504) 592-4550.

Throughout the year there are seminars and conferences sponsored by a variety of organizations, each devoted to different aspects of trading. The content of most of these seminars is not directed to beginners, however. Nevertheless, it's important that you know about these seminars as you set your long-range goals:

- American Management Association (800) 262-9699
- Blanchard & Co., Inc. (800) 880-4653
- Emerging Markets Trading Association (617) 270-6200
- FIA—Futures Industry Association (202) 466-5460
- FII—Futures Industry Institute (202) 223-1528
- FOW—Futures and Options World 001-071+827-9977
- ISI—Investment Seminars Inc. (800) 226-0323

- MAR—Managed Account Reports (212) 213-6202
- MFA—Managed Futures Association (415) 325-3133
- Morningstar (312) 696-6000
- MTA—Market Technicians Association (212) 912-0995
- NIBA—National Introducing Brokers Association (312) 977-0598
- NYMEX—New York Mercantile Exchange (212) 938-2222
- Reuters (617) 270-6200
- Risk Management Conferences (800) OPTIONS
- SAAFTI—Society of Asset Allocators and Fund Timers, Inc. (303) 989-5656.

In addition, many of the exchanges offer seminars and workshops which are educational in nature. Contact their public relations department or their library for specific information:

- CBOE—Chicago Board Options Exchange (800) OPTIONS
- CBOT—Chicago Board of Trade (800) THE-CBOT
- CME—Chicago Mercantile Exchange (312) 930-8236
- LIFFE—London International Financial Futures & Options Exchange (212) 385-1515.
- NYFE—New York Futures Exchange (800) 843-6933

8   CHARLATANS AND THEIR TECHNIQUES

While it is not necessary that we devote very much space to this topic, it is important that it be briefly addressed. In all endeavors THAT involve the exchange of money, there is always someone who wants a free lunch, and is willing to cheat to get it. Standing in the bushes is Little Red Riding Hood's wolf, ready to take advantage of the unsuspecting.

In your analysis of any purchase keep in mind that anything which seems too good to be true probably is. If you are looking for a free lunch, you'll probably get it handed to you on a plate.

Trading is a difficult business THAT takes many years to learn and many failures to teach you the lessons. You cannot expect to step up to the plate for the first time and hit a home run.

Be suspicious of advertisements which guarantee you thousands of percent profit for no work on your part. Be wary of vendors who promise you instant success. Do your homework before you purchase any software, newsletter, fax service, trading system, or seminar.

Some time ago a subscriber of my magazine, *Traders' Catalog & Resource Guide*, called to say that he would be willing to pay $10,000 for every trading system he could find which was profitable. His only condition was that he be given the system in *TradeStation* format, password protected, so that he could conduct the back-testing himself. This caller wanted to place a classified ad to this effect in the upcoming issue of *TC&RG*. I told him I would not take the ad, and further warned him that he could lose a lot of money on this venture. Unconvinced, he wanted to know how this was possible, since he would be personally conducting the testing.

Creating a system which works in the past is very simple. Creating a system which works in the future is an enormous project indeed. But he didn't ask for a system that works in the future. I explained to this caller that I could simply take the known data for the S&P 500 from 1982 to present and pick all the highs and lows, create a database of the dates of those important price points, and generate trades based on those specific dates. Protecting the "system" with a password and selling it to him to test would generate outstanding results. But it would never work for any future trades and he would be out $10,000.

Since I thought of that little "sure thing" system off the top of my head, I can only assume that there are clever people out there who can generate many more schemes to liberate you from your cash.

Don't Let the Goblins Get You

There are several ways you can locate information about products or services in which you are interested, sort of like a *Consumer Reports* for traders. Several companies have established their businesses around tracking the performance of other peoples' businesses.

If you are considering the purchase of a trading system, call John Hill at *Futures Truth*, where they test publicly offered trading systems and rank their performance. For a small fee ($30 at the time of this printing) you can purchase the latest ranking information reporting on more than 150 systems, which could save you from tremendous losses.

> John Hill
> **Futures Truth**
> 815 Hillside Rd
> Hendersonville, NC 28739
> 1-704-697-0273   fax 1-704-692-7375

Another source of valuable information is *Club 3000*, where Bo Thunman publishes, in newsletter format, the compilation of commentary from users all over the world who are offering their insights and comments about vendors and systems with which they have experience.

> Bo Thunman
> **Club 3000**
> 4550 N 38th St
> Augusta, MI 49012
> 1-616-731-5600 fax 1-616-731-5600

If you are considering subscribing to an advisory newsletter, you might want to know the author's track record before you do so. For fourteen years Mark Hulbert has followed the performance of the recommendations collected in 400 portfolios. And he gives you objective performance figures in his publication.

> Mark Hulbert
> **Hulbert Financial Digest**
> 316 Commerce St
> Alexandria, VA 22314
> 1-703-683-5905 fax 1-703-836-5866

Looking for a professional money manager? Before completing the transaction, check the following sources for statistics on the traders you are considering:

> *The Barclay Institutional Report*
> Sol Waksman
> **Barclay Trading Group, Ltd.**
> 508 N 2nd St, Ste 201
> Fairfield, IA 52556-2464
> 1-800-338-2827 fax 1-515-472-9514

> *Quarterly Performance Report*
> Lois Peltz
> **MAR - Managed Account Reports**
> 220 Fifth Ave, 19th Flr
> New York, NY 10001
> 1-212-213-6202 fax 1-212-213-1870

The Stark Report
The Norwood Index Report
Stark Research, Inc.
200 W Adams, Ste 1510
Chicago, IL 60606
1-800-591-5886 fax 1-312-407-5798

Looking for just the right mutual fund? Consult first with:

Morningstar Mutual Funds
Morningstar, Inc.
225 West Wacker Dr
Chicago, IL 60606
1-800-876-5005 fax 1-312-696-6001

And then you can do comparison shopping.

If it's stocks you're looking for, do your comparison shopping with the ultimate research tool:

Value Line Investment Survey
Value Line
71 3rd Ave
New York, NY 10017-4064
1-800-634-3583 fax 1-212-338-9623

Above all, don't get caught unprepared. Do your homework before you buy.

Further Reading

Where Are the Customer's Yachts? by Fred Schwed, Jr.
Den of Thieves by James B. Stewart

9 WHAT DO YOU TRADE?

Introduction

Don't buy something you can't sell.

Before trading anything, you need to be certain that there is a liquid market for it. Your condominium may be worth jillions on paper, but if you can't get rid of it, it is really worth nothing.

Look at the volume and number of shares of a stock being traded before you jump in. If it's futures you're trading, first consult the "Trading Liquidity" table in each issue of *Technical Analysis of Stocks and Commodities* magazine. If the liquidity is high, you'll be able to get in and out of your trades; if not, you might get stuck.

Trading Vehicles

Bonds

Bonds are simply loans which you are making to someone else: government bonds, corporate bonds and municipal bonds are examples. The certificate for that bond shows the interest rate you are being paid, the maturity of the loan and the par value (the amount you'll be paid when the loan is over). The bond certificate is negotiable, that is it can be exchanged for cash, so they belong in a safe, yours or your broker's.

There are two ways you can make a profit trading bonds: on the coupon (the interest rate) and on the appreciation of the bond itself. If you purchase a five-year $1,000 bond at par ($1,000) with a 7 percent coupon, you'll not only get your $1,000 back at the end of the five-years, you'll receive 7 percent interest per year in the meantime. If you purchase a five-year $1,000 bond at par with a 7 percent coupon, and during the holding period the value of the bond rises you can sell it at a profit before it matures. When making this decision, you will weigh the benefits of receiving the profit now against the total interest you would earn by holding the bond to maturity.

Bonds seem pretty safe, and are considered a conservative investment, but don't forget that to make income you must assume risk. The risk with bonds is that the maker (the government or municipality or corporation) will default on the loan. It doesn't happen often, but it does happen. There are ratings services like Moodys and Standard and Poors that evaluate the bonds for quality and safety and assign ratings like B, A, AA, AAA. Check a bond's rating before you buy.

Cash

In times of uncertainty cash is king. It is always wise to keep a portion of your portfolio in cash, but how much? Harry Browne's book *Why the Best-Laid Investment Plans Usually Go Wrong* is probably the best book to start with when beginning to set up your portfolio mix. Harry gives a thorough but easy to understand guide to creating both a permanent and a speculative portfolio and helps you analyze how much of your assets to assign to each. Use his guidelines as a starting point, and do your own testing on the concepts.

Futures (Commodities and Financials)

"Futures trading is speculative and includes risk of loss." The CFTC and the NFA require that all commodities trading advisors (CTAs) include this statement in any material they send out. They require this statement with good reason. The ability to trade large dollar contracts with small dollar outlay (margin) magnifies any gains or losses you might experience. Because commodities are traded on margin, people say they are very volatile. That's not quite true; if you traded each and every commodity contract for its full cash value, it wouldn't really be volatile. The size of the move you observe depends on the power of the magnifying glass you use.

Futures trading offers a unique high-risk, high-return investment medium for seasoned traders. Don't ever lose sight of the fact that it's like buying a $100,000 house with $5,000. To further complicate the deal, futures contracts expire. That is, you are obligated to complete your transaction within a specified period of time. With this in mind, it's like buying that house and knowing you must sell it within the next three months.

All the basics of futures trading are presented in *Getting Started in Futures* by Todd Lofton. Todd does a great job of explaining everything you need to know to get started, including an in-depth look at each of the futures contracts.

Mutual Funds

A mutual fund is like a cooperative: a group of investors pooling their money can purchase stocks, bonds, or other investments that each alone could not afford. The mutual fund is managed by a professional investment company; you pay these people a fee for structuring and running the "collective" for you. Developed in 1924, mutual funds have grown to have specialties like stock index funds, gold funds, bond funds, and more.

As a trader, you can time the market, time the economy or time sectors within the economy and buy and sell mutual funds to take advantage of these moves. The advantage to you is that you can usually participate with a much smaller cash outlay than trading the stock, bond, or futures directly. The disadvantage is that you will have to pay fees to the management company as well as brokerage fees to buy and sell the mutual fund.

In the analysis of mutual funds, you'll want to gather your data, chart it historically and follow the same process as if you were trading a stock, bond or futures contract. You will still be looking for a system to reveal buy and sell opportunities, testing your system exhaustively and following the system once it's developed.

Many mutual fund management companies permit **switching**, although some funds have disallowed the practice. Mutual fund switching means that you have established an account which stays at that particular management company, where they have several funds, say sector funds, a gold fund, and a stock fund. Presumably they also have a money market fund that allows you to put your money in cash rather than in any of the designated funds. Your analysis of each fund shows buying and selling opportunities, you can move your money out of one fund and into another, usually without incurring much more than a small transfer fee. This is called switching, because you are switching your money back and forth between funds while keeping it at one management company.

Mutual Fund Switch Strategies & Timing Tactics by Warren Boroson is one of the Investor's Self-Teaching Seminars by Probus Publishing. This book will lead you through the step-by-step process of learning to trade mutual funds by timing and switching.

Options

Often thought to be the "safe" way to trade, options are about as safe as skydiving. Yeah, you've got a parachute, but your time frame for using it is limited.

Options can be considered portfolio insurance, or they can be used as a purely speculative venture on their own.

Let's start with an example. You own 100 shares of IBM, which you bought at 50. IBM is now selling for 100. The market seems to be vulnerable and you don't want to lose your profit. Since you are not certain that the market will continue to go up, you can purchase **put options** on IBM which will act as insurance. If the price of IBM goes down, the value of your options goes up, theoretically covering the loss in the stock.

Definitions:

Put Option
A put option is a contract that allows an owner to **sell** a fixed number of underlying security of futures contracts at a fixed price and a fixed time period.

Call Option

A contract that gives the **buyer** of the option the right, but not the obligation, to take delivery of the underlying security at a specific price within a certain time.

That seems simple enough: if you have a put option, you want the price of the underlying stock to go down; if you have a call option you want the price of the underlying stock to go up. So where's the risk?

The value of an option decays with time. As the time for the option to expire approaches, the speculative value decreases. If the value of the option were the linear inverse of the price of the stock, one's straight line upward would be matched with the other's straight line downward, but that's not the case. (See Figure 9.1)

The risk is that you will have properly determined the direction of the market and nevertheless lose the **premium** (the money you paid for the option) because it will expire before the market reaches your goal.

This is not pencil and calculator stuff. To watch the ever-volatile options market and factor in all the variables requires a computer and a software package which specializes in options. OptionVue and Optionomics both have software for this purpose. Institute for Options Research, Inc. and Options Institute have software, books, and training for options trading.

David L. Caplan, of Opportunities in Options, authored a 45-page pamphlet, which you can get for free just by calling him. The pamphlet, entitled *Profiting with Futures Options*, gives four tables which we find

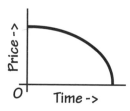

Figure 9.1   Time Value of Options

particularly valuable for options traders. We reproduce the tables here for your reference. For a quick overview of options trading we suggest you contact Mr. Caplan. for the pamphlet.

Common Option Strategies for All Markets

Option Spread Strategy	Position	Characteristics	Best Time to Use
Neutral Strategies			
Neutral Option Position	Sell out-of-money put and call	Maximum use of time value decay	Trading range market with volatility peaking
Guts	Sell in-the-money put and call	Receive large premium	Options have time value premium and market in trading range
Arbitrage	Purchase and sell similar options simultaneously	Profit certain if done at credit	Any time when credit is received
Conversion	Buy futures, buy at-the-money put and sell out-of-the money call	Profit certain if done at credit	Any time when credit is received
Box	Sell calls and puts same strike price	Profit certain if done at credit	Any time when credit is received
Butterfly	Buy at-the-money call (put) sell 2 out-of-the-money calls (puts) and buy out-of-money call (put)	Profit certain if done at credit	Any time when credit is received
Calendar	Sell near month, buy far mnth, same strike price	Near month time value will decay faster	Small debit, trading range market

Mixed Strategies

Ratio Call	Buy call, sell calls of higher strike price	Neutral, slightly bullish	Large credit and difference between strike prices of option bought and sold
Ratio Put	Buy put, sell puts of lower strike price	Neutral, slightly bearish	Large credit and difference between strike prices of option bought and sold
Straddle Purchase	Buy put and call	Options will lose time value premium quickly	Options under-valued and market likely to make a big move
Covered Call	Buy futures, sell call	Collect premium on calls sold	Neutral—slightly bullish
Covered Put	Sell futures, sell put	Collect premium on puts sold	Neutral—slightly bearish

Bullish Strategies

Buy Call	Most bullish option position	Loss limited	Undervalued option with volatility increasing
Sell Put	Neutral—bullish option position	Profit limited	Option over-valued, market flat to bullish
Vertical Bull—Call	Buy call, sell call of higher strike price	Loss limited	Small debit, bullish market
Vertical Bull—Puts	Buy put, sell put of higher strike price	Loss limited	Large credit, bullish market

Bearish Strategies

Buy Put	Most bearish option position	Loss limited	Undervalued option with increasing volatility

Sell Call	Neutral—bearish option position	Profit limited	Option over-valued , market flat, bearish
Vertical Bear—Puts	Buy at-the-money put, sell in-the-money put	Loss limited	Small debit, bearish market
Vertical Bear—Calls	Sell call, buy calls at higher strike price	Loss limited	Large credit, bearish market

There are two books you must read before trading options: *Getting Started in Options* by Michael C. Thomsett and *Options as a Strategic Investment* by Lawrence G. McMillan. The first book is an easy-reading, how-to guide to getting started in options trading. After you understand this one, get a copy of the second book to study. McMillan's book is thorough and complex, but is the definitive work on options trading. I'm often asked where to find formulas for options trading, specifically the Black-Scholes equations; it's all in McMillan.

Stocks

When you buy a share of stock you are becoming an owner of the company who issued the stock. That's putting it simply, but all too often we forget there is a company and a product behind our trade.

Don't take hot tips from friends or brokers; stock trading is not a game. If you are a fundamental analyst, do your research on the company you're buying; if you're a technician, analyze your charts.

Stock picking can be an arduous task. There are over 6,000 stocks from which you can pick. One way to approach this monumental task is with computer software. Technifilter Plus, FirstAlert, and Telescan offer you methods to specify parameters to search for and let the computer do the scanning. For instance, you might want to narrow your analysis to only those stocks whose price is 3 percent higher than it was last month, or to stocks which are below their 50-day moving average. Again, any theory you develop about what makes individual stock prices move must be thoroughly tested. Don't make the mistake of thinking that stock trading is simpler or less risky and trying to skip your homework.

There are lots and lots of books you can read about the stock market. I suggest you start with *The Intelligent Investor* by Benjamin Graham and then read *The Stock Market* by Richard Teweles.

Investment Timing

Timing is everything. You buy the right stuff at the right time, you make money. You buy the right stuff at the wrong time, you lose money.

One book stands out above all the rest when it comes to the broad picture of timing: *Strategic Investment Timing* by Dick A. Stoken. This book is an in-depth, but easy to understand, analysis of long-term timing strategies. Dick addresses economic cycles and methods of profiting from each phase. He shows you when to buy and sell stocks and bonds, when to have your assets in cash, when to trade commodities, when to buy and sell real estate.

Contrary Investing

Contrary investing means you figure out what everyone else is doing and you do the opposite.

> *Buy when everyone else is selling, and hold until everyone else is buying. This is more than just a catchy slogan. It is the very essence of successful investment.*
>
> —J. Paul Getty, "How to Be Rich"

This is all well and good if you have a way of telling what everyone else is doing. For the most part, aggressive contrary investing is tantamount to predicting tops and bottoms; it can't be done. To be successful as a contrarian you need to be able to scale into your trades and be able to wait out the completion of the trend. For instance, contrarians started shorting the stock market in 1986. It was the right idea, but too soon. Even though it was "over-valued" the market continued up until October of 1987. To be a successful contrarian in that example you would have needed a tremendous amount of capital to continue adding to your short positions until it finally crashed.

Nevertheless, contrary advice is well headed if you are using it not to predict the future, but to avoid lemming behavior. Don't follow the crowd; be your own guru. Your studies and extensive testing will tell you what to invest in, not the mania and panic reactions of people in groups.

For a practical, common sense look at contrary investing, pick up a copy of *Contrary Investing—The Insider's Guide to Buying Low and Selling High* by Richard E. Band.

10 SELECTING A COMPUTER

PC or Macintosh?

Unless you have a scientific application which requires the power of a Cray computer, you should first choose your software, and then purchase the computer which will optimally run that software. (Crays don't come with software, you have to write your own.)

At last count there were 432 financial software products which run on PCs (IBM or compatible) and 36 financial software products which run on the Macintosh platform.

With only eight percent of the software products running on Macs, it makes sense to buy a PC, if you only look at that piece of information. But, if you have an idea what software you want to use, and what market application you are interested in and it's available on the Macintosh—then you should buy a Mac.

The American Association of Individual Investors (AAII) publishes a book called *The Individual Investor's Guide to Computerized Investing*. In the back of the book are "Investment Software Grids" which list all of the PC software and all of the Macintosh software for traders/investors.

When purchasing a new computer, buy the most you can afford with respect to processing power and disk space. Personal computers get cheaper every year, and software grows to fill the available space. My personal preference is to devote one computer to trading, and have nothing else running on it. Even though one is free to run in a multi-processing environment, I don't put anything else on my trading computer. I wouldn't want to take a chance on one piece of software having a bug which could interfere in any way with my trading software or data. (All software has bugs. It is a logical impossibility to create bug-free code.)

If you already have a computer which you want to use for your trading, and you don't want to purchase a new one, then use the AAII guide or *TC&RG* as a resource and start collecting demos. If you don't have a computer, you can rent one or use a friend's or go to a place like Kinko's Copy Center where you can use their computers. The only way you will really know what software you like is to try it.

Every decision you make should involve Benjamin Franklin's decision-tree process. Make a list of your "musts" and your "wants." What features must your trading computer have? What features would you like it to have. Create a grid and start asking questions. Go to your local computer store and window shop. Keep the pros and the cons in the grid.

You'll want to know details about cost and features. You'll want to know what the minimum computer configuration is for each software demo you've ordered. Let's say that one piece of software needs a 386 processor, 4 megabytes of memory and uses 5 megabytes of disk space on your harddrive. A second piece of software needs a pentium processor with 8 megabytes of memory and uses 30 megabytes of storage. Does bigger always mean better? Not necessarily. In this case, you'll probably be paying more for the computer and more for the software, but it doesn't necessarily mean that you will make more trading profits. (And that's our only real concern, remember?)

All of the information you get from the hardware vendors must be put into a table for you to use in your final analysis. You don't want to buy a lot more computer than you need, but at the same time, you don't want to get a computer that you will shortly outgrow.

Presented in Figure 10.1 is the format I would use while inquiring about computer hardware.

To keep from getting really confused, make sure you compare oranges with oranges. If your list includes computers of widely differing

MFGR	TOTAL PRICE	Pentium	14" VGA Color Monitor	1.44 MB 3.5" floppy drive	1 Gig. Hard Drive	16 MB RAM	CD-ROM 4x	Tape Backup

Figure 10.1 Fill in the prices for each option and add up the total.

configurations, it'll be impossible to compare price. A clean way to solve that problem is to ask each manufacturer in writing for a quote on a specific configuration.

Offhand I know of more than 50 hardware manufacturers you can call to get information. Or, if you prefer, most computer software stores carry a periodical called *Computer Shopper*, which is a huge catalog of hardware of all kinds.

List of Computer Vendors

Acer	Acma	ALR	Ambra
Apple	AST	Austin	Axik
Blackship	Canon	Compaq	CompuAdd
Compudyne	CompuTrend	Cornell	DEC
Dell	DTK	Epson	Everex
Gateway	Grid Systems	Hewlett-Packard	Hyundai
IBM	Insight	Leading Edge	Micro Express
Micron	MIS	Mitac	NCR
NEC	Northgate	Packard Bell	Panasonic
PC Brand	Prof. Technologies	Samsung	Sharp
Swan	Tandon	Tandy	Tangent
Texas Instruments	Toshiba	Tri-Star	Twinhead
Unisys	USA Flex	Wang	Wyse
Zenith	Zeos		

11 SELECTING SOFTWARE

Introduction

The software you choose for your data analysis and system testing is your toolbox. It is not the end of your thinking and theorizing, it is the beginning. Some people think that when they finally get to the software stage that they are done, that the computer will do the thinking for them. Not so.

Computers will never (mark my word) take the place of the human brain. That's a sci-fi fantasy perpetuated by people who don't understand how computers work. A computer is limited by the human who is conceptualizing and programming it. It will not reach out on its own and imagine new scenarios.

The human brain can imagine. Furthermore, each and every human brain imagines differently. It is this diversity of imagination that makes the market. Some people think it is time to sell while others think it is time to buy. I have talked with hundreds, maybe even thousands, of traders and never once found that any one of them had the same system as any other. In fact, no two have even agreed on what moves the market.

The software we're addressing in this chapter is the kind which will be the tool for your imagination to use in simplifying calculations and charting. A computer really is just a very fast adding machine. We use it in trading to make our lives easier, so we don't have to sit and watch the ticker tape with pen and paper in hand making manual calculations. The computer can do all this much faster. Nevertheless, it will only do what you tell it to.

It is very easy to allow the software selection process to become your main focus and to let your trading become secondary. If software analysis becomes your goal, and not the means to your goal, change your job title from trader to software reviewer.

The search for better and better software will not necessarily improve your trading. Buying a better camera will not make you a better photographer. You can become a better photographer by taking classes and practicing; you can become a better trader by taking classes and practicing. Good classes in photography are more readily available than good classes in trading, so for the most part you will be reading and studying on your own.

Software selection presumes that you already have determined your trading focus. If you focus on trading options you will want different software than if you focus on trading mutual funds. If you focus on trading commodity futures you will want different software from either of the above.

If you go to your local computer store looking for software, you won't find much. Very few of the trading products have made it to the shelves. From that perspective you would think that no such software is available. That couldn't be further from the truth. There are, at my last count, 432 software products which are specifically directed to investing and trading. They just aren't in the computer stores.

You find trading software in special interest magazines, catalogs and resource guides. I keep the most up-to-date list of all trading software products in *TC&RG* and on the Internet at *The Money Mentor*, along with descriptions and reviews. For the most part, trading software is acquired by mail-order. If you go to trade shows and conferences related to trading, you can usually find many of the vendors there with their latest products and demonstration units they'll be happy to show you. Otherwise, you call the vendor, ask for a demo disk if they have one, try that out for a day or two, and then order the software over the phone.

Again, every decision you make should involve Benjamin Franklin's decision-tree process. Make a list of your "musts" and your "wants". What features **must** your trading software have? What features would you **like** (or want) it to have. Create a grid and start using each of the demos you've ordered. As you use the software, write down what's good about it and what's bad about it. Keep the pros and the cons in the grid.

I like to assign a value from 0 to 10 to each item under consideration, with 0 being "worthless" and 10 being "must." That way, when you've completed the grid, you can add up all the numbers and have a simple value comparison.

For instance, here's a simple table to begin with:

Program Name: _____

Ease of Use	(0 - 10)	_____
Technical Indicators	(0 - 10)	_____
Computational Speed	(0 - 10)	_____
Graphics Capabilities	(0 - 10)	_____
Documentation	(0 - 10)	_____
Customer Support	(0 - 10)	_____

When I first began my research, I made a spreadsheet with every feature of every demo I ordered and compared them all to each other in great detail. I continue to update that table, and from time to time I publish it in *TC&RG* or on the Internet. Doing the work yourself will give you a much better idea of the functionality of each demo, and how comfortable you are with its workings. It's much too extensive to publish here, but if you'd like to look at the research I've done, feel free to check either source; it's updated every six months or so.

Later in this book we discuss "canned" trading systems, that is systems which someone else has developed and which you purchase. This chapter is not for that. Here we will take a quick look at some of the bestselling software products which can assist you in your development of your own trading system.

Fitness for Purpose

You can get financial software that will address nearly any aspect of the markets in which you are interested. The software which is general in nature, and of mass-market interest, is inexpensive; software which is designed for a narrow, specific audience is usually very expensive.

In the beginning of your trading career, it makes sense to acquire software with which you can grow and learn. Two popular products are available which will get you started for minimal dollar outlay and from which you can expand to their professional products at a later time.

MetaStock for Windows, a product of Equis International (1-800-882-3040 x55), runs on IBM and compatible computers. MetaStock is clean, simple, and intuitive. You can install it in just a few minutes and begin using it right away. *MetaStock* is Microsoft Office Compatible, a high standard to meet, and is object oriented. By that I mean you can click on an object, like a moving average, and drag it to another chart. You don't have to go through a maze of computerese set-up steps. *MetaStock* provides more technical analysis indicators than you could possibly ever need, as well as a simple development language for creating your own indicators and testing your system ideas.

Equis International offers a variety of companion products for traders, including *The Downloader, The Technician, Pulse, MetaStock Real-Time,* and a host of educational products. When your trading moves from the learning stage to the professional stage, you can graduate into *MetaStock Real-Time* without losing all the work you've done in *MetaStock.*

SuperCharts, from Omega Research (1-800-556-2022 x1081C), is also a Windows product, running on IBMs and clones. The big brother of *SuperCharts* is called *TradeStation,* and is their real-time analysis product. Both of these products are easy to install and intuitive to use. Both use Omega's *Easy Language* for developing your own systems and indicators.

Both *MetaStock* and *SuperCharts* run between $300—$400. Frankly, as a software designer, I don't know how either of them can sell such powerful analysis software so inexpensively. Each has a tremendous amount of man-time and research behind them.

Newer to the technical analysis software shelves are two products, one for Macintosh and one for Windows. *TickerWatcher,* by Linn Software, is for Macs and is impressive in its scope. It provides real-time, delayed, or end-of-day analysis, portfolio management, and screening in addition to the vast array of technical analysis tools and magnificent charting capabilities. *TickerWatcher* ranges in price from $395 to $695, depending on the optional extras you choose.

Heir to the CompuTrac tradition, *SMARTrader* is an all purpose, easy-to-use technical analysis software program for Windows, developed by former employees of the erstwhile CompuTrac. Intuitive and simple in design, *SMARTrader* has all the bells and whistles and at its introductory price of $199 is the least expensive of the four.

Worden Brothers, Inc. makes their technical analysis software, *TeleChart 2000*, available for next to nothing. It usually is available for $29, although I've seen it as low as $19.95. So how do they stay in business?? You get your data from them—and even that's incredibly cheap. Their data runs anywhere from $2.50 per month to $19 per month. While *TeleChart 2000* is not available in a real-time version, their end-of-day technical analysis is quite respectable.

The four other software products mentioned in this chapter require an outside vendor for your data transmission, whether it be end-of-day or real-time. See the next chapter for a list of data sources and compatible software.

Throwaways

All of the software mentioned above is so inexpensive in the overall scheme of things, that you can begin with any one of them and throw them away when you are ready to graduate. This is not to say that you will need to do so, as each of them is sufficient for advanced analysis. But, if you spend the early part of your education with these products and find that you want to specialize in a more narrow facet of trading, you certainly haven't wasted your money. Everything you learn with these products will be applicable throughout your trading career.

I could write volumes on the myriad of software products available to traders, but others have beat me to it and you should benefit from their expert analysis. Four books come to mind which are devoted to the exposition of trading software:

- *The Individual Investor's Guide to Computerized Investing* is updated annually by The American Association of Individual Investors, a nonprofit educational organization. In this guide you can find a complete list of products and descriptions, along with prices and phone numbers.

- Chuck LeBeau and David Lucas coauthored *Computer Analysis of the Futures Market*, addressing practical ways to use the most common technical studies. They examine which studies to combine for greater profits, which signals to trade and which need to be confirmed. The book also delves into uses of popular analysis software such as MetaStock, Telescan, SuperCharts and more.

- *The Stock Market Investor's Computer Guide*, by Michael Gianturco, explains in clear, simple English the pros and cons of a wide range of computer hardware and software, as well as offering a clear explanation of what computers can and cannot do.

- Bruce Babcock's *The Dow Jones-Irwin Guide to Trading Systems* offers both an analysis of trading software and a comprehensive look at developing your own system. You should put this book on your "must" reading list, just after you've finished all the books in the beginners section and just before you begin your software selection process.

The following table is one I update and publish in *TC&RG* every six months or so. As with my other research, I also make this table available at my Internet site, in its most up-to-date configuration. This table began years ago as my first decision-tree analysis of trading software. It has expanded greatly since then, including the widest range of software and capabilities you can imagine. Studying this table will save you months and months of work. Note that I'm only including a few of the vast number of vendors, due to the space limitations of this book. If you want to see the full list, come to *The Money Mentor* on the Internet, where paper is not a limitation.

Software Comparison Table

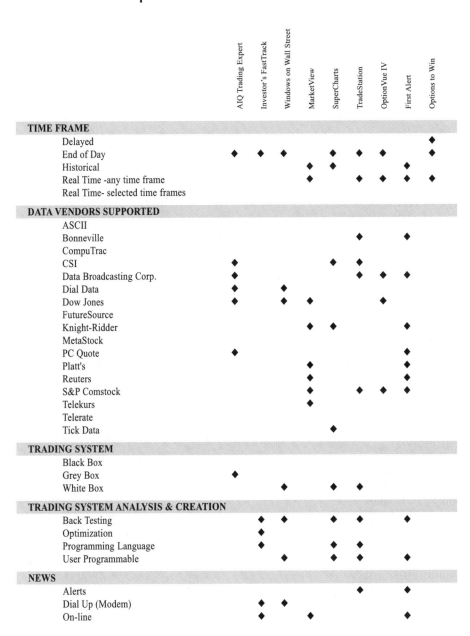

	AIQ Trading Expert	Investor's FastTrack	Windows on Wall Street	MarketView	SuperCharts	TradeStation	OptionVue IV	First Alert	Options to Win
TIME FRAME									
Delayed									◆
End of Day	◆	◆	◆		◆	◆	◆	◆	◆
Historical				◆	◆			◆	
Real Time -any time frame				◆	◆	◆		◆	◆
Real Time- selected time frames									
DATA VENDORS SUPPORTED									
ASCII									
Bonneville						◆		◆	
CompuTrac									
CSI	◆				◆	◆			
Data Broadcasting Corp.	◆					◆	◆	◆	
Dial Data	◆		◆						
Dow Jones	◆		◆	◆			◆		
FutureSource									
Knight-Ridder					◆	◆		◆	
MetaStock									
PC Quote	◆							◆	
Platt's					◆			◆	
Reuters					◆			◆	
S&P Comstock					◆		◆	◆	
Telekurs					◆				
Telerate									
Tick Data					◆				
TRADING SYSTEM									
Black Box									
Grey Box	◆								
White Box			◆		◆	◆			
TRADING SYSTEM ANALYSIS & CREATION									
Back Testing		◆	◆		◆	◆		◆	
Optimization		◆							
Programming Language		◆			◆	◆			
User Programmable			◆		◆	◆		◆	
NEWS									
Alerts							◆	◆	
Dial Up (Modem)		◆	◆						
On-line		◆		◆				◆	

	AIQ Trading Expert	Investor's FastTrack	Windows on Wall Street	MarketView	SuperCharts	TradeStation	OptionVue IV	First Alert	Options to Win
ACCOUNT MANAGEMENT									
Client Account Management	◆			◆			◆	◆	
Personal Account Management	◆						◆	◆	
Performance Summary	◆	◆			◆	◆	◆	◆	
Positions Log	◆	◆		◆	◆	◆	◆	◆	
Statistical Analysis		◆			◆	◆	◆		
Variable # contracts					◆	◆	◆	◆	◆
MONEY MANAGEMENT									
Optimal-f									
Portfolio Management				◆				◆	
What-if Analysis							◆		
NEURAL NETWORK									
Back Propagation									
Excel Interface									
ALERTS									
Calendar							◆		
News & Information									
Price	◆						◆	◆	
Time	◆						◆		
Volume	◆						◆	◆	
SPREADSHEET INTERFACE									
ASCII text file	◆	◆							
DDE Link							◆	◆	
Excel		◆					◆	◆	
Lotus		◆						◆	
TOOLS									
% Retracement			◆		◆	◆			◆
Anble of Trendline					◆	◆			◆
Andrews Pitchfork			◆						◆
Channels	◆		◆		◆	◆			◆
Cycle Arcs					◆				◆
Cycle Lines			◆		◆	◆			◆
Ellipse					◆				◆
Fibonacci Fan Lines			◆		◆	◆			◆
Fibonacci Time Zones			◆		◆	◆			◆
Gann Angles			◆		◆	◆			◆
Horizontal Lines			◆		◆	◆			◆
Linear Regression			◆		◆	◆			◆
Parallel Lines					◆	◆			◆
Rectangles					◆	◆			◆
Speed/Resistance Lines			◆		◆	◆			◆
Standard Deviation		◆	◆		◆	◆			◆

	AIQ Trading Expert	Investor's FastTrack	Windows on Wall Street	MarketView	SuperCharts	TradeStation	OptionVue IV	First Alert	Options to Win
Support/Resistance			♦		♦	♦		♦	
Text'			♦		♦	♦		♦	
Trend Lines	♦	♦	♦		♦	♦		♦	

INDICATORS

	AIQ Trading Expert	Investor's FastTrack	Windows on Wall Street	MarketView	SuperCharts	TradeStation	OptionVue IV	First Alert	Options to Win
Accumulation Swing Index			♦	♦	♦	♦			
Accumulation-Distribution	♦		♦		♦	♦		♦	
ADX	♦		♦		♦	♦		♦	
Alpha Beta Trend									
Andrews' Pitchfork			♦					♦	
Arms Ease of Movement									
Arms Equivolume									
Average Range Channel					♦	♦		♦	
Average True Range		♦		♦	♦	♦		♦	
Baskets - user definable				♦	♦	♦		♦	
Bollinger Bands	♦		♦		♦	♦		♦	
Chaikin Oscillator			♦						
Commodity Channel Index	♦		♦		♦	♦	♦	♦	
Commodity Selection			♦		♦	♦			
Correlation Analysis								♦	
Daily Range			♦	♦	♦	♦		♦	
Demand Index			♦						
Detrended Price Oscillator		♦	♦	♦		♦		♦	
Difference Line					♦	♦		♦	
Dividend Yield Matrix		♦						♦	
Division Line			♦						
DMI (Directional Movement)	♦		♦	♦	♦	♦		♦	
Equivolume	♦							♦	
Fibonacci Movement			♦		♦	♦		♦	
Fourier Transform									
Gapless Bar Chart					♦	♦			
Hal Momentum									
Herrick Payoff Index			♦		♦	♦			
Japanese Candlesticks	♦		♦		♦	♦		♦	
Key Reversal					♦	♦			
MACD	♦	♦	♦		♦	♦		♦	
Market Profile				♦				♦	
Mass Index			♦						
McClellan Oscillator	♦				♦	♦			
McClellan Summation Index	♦								
Median Price			♦		♦	♦		♦	
MFI	♦		♦		♦	♦		♦	
Momentum	♦	♦	♦	♦	♦	♦		♦	
Momentum Oscillator	♦	♦	♦	♦	♦	♦		♦	
Money Flow Index	♦		♦		♦	♦		♦	

103

	AIQ Trading Expert	Investor's FastTrack	Windows on Wall Street	MarketView	SuperCharts	TradeStation	OptionVue IV	First Alert	Options to Win
Moving Average - 1 line	◆		◆	◆	◆	◆		◆	
Moving Average - 2 lines			◆	◆	◆	◆		◆	
Moving Average - 3 lines			◆	◆	◆	◆		◆	
Moving Average - Displaced			◆		◆	◆			
Moving Average - Envelopes			◆		◆	◆		◆	
Moving Average - Exponential		◆	◆	◆	◆	◆		◆	
Moving Average - Weighted			◆		◆	◆		◆	
Negative Volume Index	◆		◆						
On Balance Volume	◆		◆	◆	◆	◆		◆	
Open Interest	◆		◆	◆	◆	◆		◆	
Option Analysis	◆			◆				◆	
Overlays - differenc technical stucies			◆		◆	◆		◆	
Overlays - different markets			◆		◆	◆		◆	
Overlays - different time frames					◆	◆		◆	
Overlays - different values of same study			◆		◆	◆		◆	
PaintBar					◆	◆			
Parabolic SAR			◆	◆	◆	◆		◆	
Percent Change	◆		◆		◆	◆		◆	
Percent R			◆	◆	◆	◆		◆	
Pivot Points					◆	◆			
Point & Figure			◆	◆	◆	◆		◆	
Positive Volume Index	◆		◆						
Price & Volume Trend	◆		◆					◆	
Price Channel					◆	◆		◆	
Printing	◆		◆	◆	◆	◆		◆	
Range Leaders					◆	◆			
Rate of Change			◆		◆	◆		◆	
Ratio									
Regression			◆		◆	◆		◆	
RSI	◆	◆	◆	◆	◆	◆		◆	
Speed/Resistance			◆		◆	◆		◆	
Spread			◆	◆	◆	◆		◆	
Standard Deviation	◆	◆	◆	◆	◆	◆		◆	
Stochastic - Fast	◆	◆	◆	◆	◆	◆		◆	
Stochastic - Slow	◆	◆	◆	◆	◆	◆		◆	
Stochastic - variable %K, %D	◆	◆	◆		◆	◆		◆	
Swing Accumulation									
Swing High/Swing Low			◆		◆	◆			
Swing Index			◆	◆	◆	◆			
Swing SAR									
Theoretical Value	◆							◆	
Tick Size (incremental volume)				◆	◆	◆		◆	
Tick Volume				◆	◆	◆		◆	
Time & Sales (tick chart)				◆	◆	◆		◆	
Time Series Forecast									

	AIQ Trading Expert	Investor's FastTrack	Windows on Wall Street	MarketView	SuperCharts	TradeStation	OptionVue IV	First Alert	Options to Win
Trade Volume Index					◆				
Trendlines	◆	◆	◆	◆	◆	◆		◆	
TRIX			◆						
Ultimate Oscillator			◆		◆	◆		◆	
Up/Dowb Average			◆	◆	◆	◆		◆	
Up/Down Tick Difference				◆	◆	◆		◆	
Vol %	◆								
Volatility SAR			◆		◆	◆		◆	
Volatility, Historical	◆				◆			◆	
Volume	◆		◆	◆	◆	◆		◆	
Volume Accumulation/Dist	◆								
Volume Oscillator	◆		◆		◆	◆		◆	
Volume Rate-of-Change			◆		◆	◆			
Weighted Close			◆		◆	◆		◆	
What-if Analysis	◆	◆				◆		◆	
Williams Ultimate Oscillator									
Williams' %R	◆		◆		◆	◆			
Zig-Zag	◆		◆		◆	◆			
DATA MAINTENANCE									
Automated	◆	◆	◆	◆			◆	◆	◆
Continuous Contract				◆	◆	◆			
Edit	◆		◆	◆	◆	◆			
Manual	◆		◆	◆	◆	◆			
Merge	◆		◆	◆	◆	◆			
Translation/Format Converter	◆	◆	◆	◆	◆	◆			
GRAPHICS									
Color	◆	◆	◆	◆	◆	◆	◆		◆
Date & Time Axis	◆		◆	◆	◆	◆			◆
Date Axis		◆	◆		◆	◆			◆
Date Axis forward in time									◆
Fonts, variable			◆		◆	◆			◆
Grids, variable			◆		◆	◆			◆
Multiple Monitors					◆	◆			◆
Multiple Windows/Charts			◆	◆	◆	◆			◆
Overlay CHarts			◆		◆	◆			◆
Overlays of Differing Time Frames					◆	◆			◆
Quote Window						◆			◆
SYSTEM LIBRARY									
Borland C									
Library Functions					◆				
OPERATING SYSTEM									
DOS	◆	◆		◆					
Macintosh									

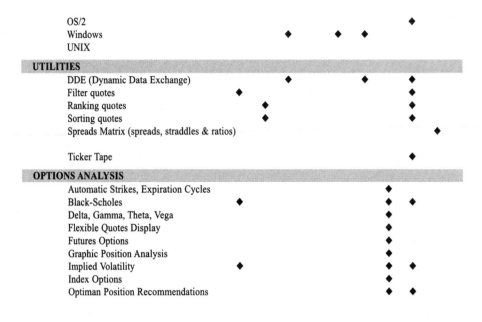

OS/2					♦
Windows		♦	♦	♦	
UNIX					
UTILITIES					
DDE (Dynamic Data Exchange)		♦		♦	♦
Filter quotes	♦				♦
Ranking quotes		♦			♦
Sorting quotes		♦			♦
Spreads Matrix (spreads, straddles & ratios)					♦
Ticker Tape					♦
OPTIONS ANALYSIS					
Automatic Strikes, Expiration Cycles				♦	
Black-Scholes	♦			♦	♦
Delta, Gamma, Theta, Vega				♦	
Flexible Quotes Display				♦	
Futures Options				♦	
Graphic Position Analysis				♦	
Implied Volatility	♦			♦	♦
Index Options				♦	
Optiman Position Recommendations				♦	♦

Still Confused?

If you still have questions about what computer or software to buy, give us a call. We can probably point you in the right direction.

12 SELECTING A DATA SOURCE

Introduction

Assuming that you have a proven system with a positive mathematical expectation, your data is the next most important concern. If you had the best system in the world and fed it bad data, you would lose money. Garbage in, garbage out (as programmers say).

Companies who sell data as their primary business have their reputations and continued success at stake based on the reliability and accuracy of the data they sell. Software companies who give data away as an incentive for you to purchase their software do not necessarily have the same goal as data vendors. Don't assume that data you get for free is totally accurate.

What is accurate data?

Each and every trade executed on the floor of the exchange has a transaction time, date, quantity and price. Tick data, or time-and-sales data, will have all of this information.

Definition:

Tick
The minimum fluctuation of a tradable. For example, bonds trade in 32nds, most stocks trade in eighths, S&P 500 index trades in 5 cent increments.

Your broker can provide time-and-sales (see Figure 12.1) for a small period of time, like a few minutes. If the data you purchase is accurate you will be able to compare it with time-and-sales data you can get from your broker and not find any differences.

Tick data (see Figure 12.1) is used to create time samplings of data. For instance, the open, high, low, and close of a day's trading are taken from the first tick, the highest tick, the lowest tick and the final tick of the day. A fifteen-minute bar is constructed from the first tick of that time period, and the last tick of that time period. (See Figure 12.2) If your tick data is not accurate, the longer term data will not be either.

If you are going to be using daily data (see Figure 12.3) , especially in the beginning of your learning curve, compare your data with data which is printed in the *Wall Street Journal, Investors Business Daily* or *Barrons* (see Figure 12.4). You'll have to collect data each day from one of these papers (they don't print historical data), but it will be well worth your time.

```
010195 09:11 345.00 345.05 345.00 345.05 345.10
010195 09:12 345.10 345.15 345.10
010195 09:13 345.15 345.20 345.15 345.20
010195 09:14 345.15 345.10
```

Figure 12.1 Time and Sales (Tick) Data

Date	Time	Open	High	Low	Close
010195	09:00	345.15	345.30	345.10	345.25
010195	09:15	345.25	345.50	345.10	345.35
010195	09:30	345.35	345.40	345.25	345.35

Figure 12.2 Fifteen-Minute Data

Date	Open	High	Low	Close
010195	345.15	345.30	345.10	345.25
010195	345.25	345.50	345.10	345.35
010195	345.35	345.40	345.25	345.35

Figure 12.3 Daily Data

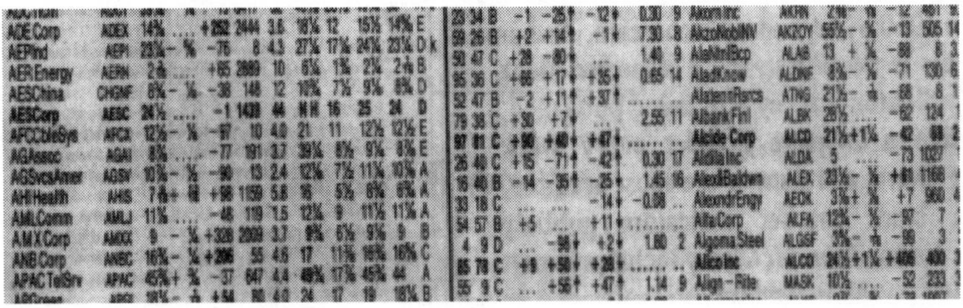

Figure 12.4 Data from Investor's Business Daily

time period, and the last tick of that time period. (See Figure 12.2) If your tick data is not accurate, the longer term data will not be either.

If you are going to be using daily data (see Figure 12.3) , especially in the beginning of your learning curve, compare your data with data which is printed in the *Wall Street Journal, Investors Business Daily* or *Barrons* (see Figure 12.4). You'll have to collect data each day from one of these papers (they don't print historical data), but it will be well worth your time.

Compare several sources of data before you lock into a single source forever. The extra step of verifying your data is as important as verifying your system.

Chapter 3 covers the sources of information and data. There is no need to repeat that material here. Referring back to Chapter 3, contact each of the data vendors for their literature and pricing, or come to *The Money Mentor* on the Internet (http://www.moneymentor.com), where we maintain a virtual home page for each of them, with information supplied to us by each vendor.

13 PURCHASING A CANNED TRADING SYSTEM

Introduction

A "canned" trading system is one which someone else has designed, hopefully tested, implemented either via computer software or an explicit manual, and now offers for sale. Most often the price of the system is in direct proportion to its efficacy. If a system is likely to make you a great deal of money, the vendor will charge you a lot for its purchase.

I break the universe of canned systems into three categories: black boxes, grey boxes and white boxes, depending on how much of the inner workings of the system are revealed to the buyer. A black box does not reveal any of the inner mechanics of the system; you buy it, you trade it blindly, that's all. The vendor of a grey box will tell you some of the theory behind what the system does, but not reveal all of its inner workings. By contrast, a white box is a fully revealed system. The vendor of a white box system will tell you everything there is to know about the way this system is designed and implemented.

The first two, black and grey boxes, will either be sold to you as a fax service, a hotline, or as software. The author cannot tell you how to trade either of these methods in a manual without revealing all the secrets. A white box can take many forms including fax services, hotlines, software, or documentation.

Confidentiality

When you purchase a system, it is important to honor your contract which usually includes a secrecy clause. Any time you purchase something intended for a single user and share it with your friends you are stealing. Furthermore, you are putting the vendor out of business. A developer can only continue to supply the market with products if he has the funds to promote research, development and marketing.

Secondly, if you contribute to the proliferation of a system by offering it to friends, you are participating in the system's demise and cutting your own throat. If enough people begin trading the same system, the system will not continue working. If everyone came to the market to buy and no one wanted to sell, because the were all looking at the same signals, that would be the end of that system.

In fact, as a student of the markets, you can see the history of market theories come and go in waves as they catch on and then fade from popularity. The wider acceptance the theory gains, the less it works. It's sort of like all the passengers running to one side of the boat.

Evaluating Canned Systems

If the vendor won't tell you how the system works, how do you know it's any good? There are several ways to answer this question. Ask the vendor for a track record of the system's historical performance. Ask whether the vendor trades that same identical system himself. Ask if you can historically test the system yourself. Contact Futures Truth and Club 3000.

The Watchdogs

Two organizations, Futures Truth and Club 3000, make it their business to know how canned systems are doing. Club 3000 was so named because at the time it seemed that most systems were selling for around $3,000. Bo Thunman, the person you'll want to contact, publishes a newsletter which is the compilation of questions and commentary sent to him by users of various systems. Bo is the conduit through which the world hears candid and heartfelt recommendations and complaints. John Hill, the founder of Futures Truth, tests hundreds of commercially available systems and then follows them in real-time trading. The Futures Truth analysis is available for a small fee, listing vendors and their performance records. In their comprehensive analysis process, Futures Truth developed their own extraordinarily powerful testing software, Excalibur, which is available for purchase as well.

If the system's so good, why are you selling pit?

This is always the most confounding question about canned systems. Of course the dilemma is that you'll get nearly the same altruistic answer from all vendors: they're doing it out of the goodness of their hearts to help you make money. The truth is they are selling it to make money, just as you are buying it to make money. Some of the systems will make money if you follow them consistently; some will lose money no matter what you do. If you do your homework you'll know which is which.

Not all composers can sing their own music. Not all systems innovators can trade. There are brilliant, prolific inventors of systems who do not have the discipline to sit in a chair day after day and execute trades; it's more fun to be outside playing golf.

Furthermore, once you get really good at trading it's boring. The exciting part of trading is in the learning stages and in the adrenaline phase when you're doing it wrong. Once your trading is systematic and mechanical it makes for a pretty dull day. At that point, you can let someone else trade the system and begin the trek again by testing new theories.

Commercially Available Systems

The following list by no means constitutes a comprehensive list of the hundreds of systems on the market. You'll get a much longer list if you contact Futures Truth and if you watch financial magazines for advertising.

Applied Fibonacci Patterns (512) 348-2996	Alpha Research & Trading
Bear, Raptor, T-Rex System (908) 906-0819	Jurasic Trading Systems
Solar Systems I & II (619) 930-1050	Sunny J. Harris
Daytrade Pro (800) 678-5253	Jake Bernstein
Time-Trend III (516) 829-6444	Gerald Appel
Pattern Probability System (407) 747-1554	Curtis Arnold
Recurrence (203) 622-8566 x 82	AVCO Financial
The Intelligent Trading System (415) 349-1668	Grant J. Renier
ProfitTaker 2000 (813) 973-0496	Louis Mendelsohn
Valentine, Volatility Tamer, Antihistamine (916) 646-1311	Bruce Babcock
Blue Monday (800) 767-2508	Joe Krutsinger

Breaking the Code

As a beginning trader there is some value to purchasing a system merely to use as an example. By watching what someone else has done you can not only begin to decipher their techniques, but you will begin to form ideas of your own with which you can experiment.

Don't waste your time trying to hack through the passwords or system protections, it's not worth your time and you risk prosecution.

Following the System

Following someone else's system is in many ways harder than following your own. When you develop your own system you understand how you set up the rules and you can often anticipate trades, because you know how it works. Even so, when you get in the inevitable period of drawdown, you will experience doubt and fear. Your discipline and confidence gained through diligent testing and research will keep you going. But, when you are blind to the methodology you have purchased it is harder to continue the faith. You have no way to know just how bad it's going to get.

Nevertheless, if you skip a trade (or several) or if you try to second-guess the system, you have cheated. If you don't follow each and every trade, you are not trading the system you purchased! If you lose money under these conditions, it's not the system's fault, it's yours. Worse yet, if you make more money than the system did you will be encouraged to continue cheating, and more than likely your guessing will eventually "smack you up side the head" with a losing streak that the system doesn't experience.

14 THE NEVER-ENDING SEARCH FOR THE HOLY GRAIL

From time immemorial we have been looking for "the answer." Humanity has continued to search for the Holy Grail generation after generation. Only the wise know that there is no answer.

In all likelihood you will not win the lottery, you will not make a killing in the stock market and Santa Claus won't bring you a cashiers check for a million dollars. Nevertheless, it seems to be human nature to keep hoping.

Novice and seasoned traders alike continue to search for just the right system, or just the right advisor so that the light will shine brightly and the answer will have been found.

I have observed many a new trader skip from technique to technique and from guru to guru as each one in turn fails to be the Holy Grail.

Forget it. You have all the answers you need within. Amaze yourself!

What you may not have is the discipline to organize your thoughts, test your ideas, and then follow them without wavering. But, don't give up too soon, these aspects of trading can be trained to some extent.

In *Zen in the Markets* Edward Allen Toppel says:

> *Most of us come to the market with the notion that if certain events happen, the market should react in this or that way. The market will go up or down because of this event. Let us call this*

Aristotelian logic and let us promptly recognize that Aristotle belongs in universities and not in markets.

Our brains are programmed with the wrong information. We need to de-program what we learned in school about balance sheets and price earnings ratios. They do not guarantee price direction.

We must realize that the market defies logic. It has a logic all of its own, and it won't tell us in advance what its reaction to events will be. We can watch for clues and then react. Basically, the best we can hope for is quick reaction time to the market's signals. We must first wait and then follow.

Approach trading like any other new career path. You wouldn't think you could become a successful surgeon without training. Neither can you become a successful (that is profitable) trader without training. Becoming a surgeon takes 10 or more years of training! How is it that new students of the markets often hope they can become traders within months?

While no one has "the answer" but you, don't forget that you can only find it with years of research and study and experimentation.

Consider every fork of every road you take to be a learning experience, and not an end to your travels.

The rules of successful trading are: think, test, and follow. These are the phases your journey must take. Think about what you see the market doing; test your theories and design your system; then follow it religiously.

Phase One—Think

Subscribe to papers and journals and newsletters. Listen to hotlines and advisors. Read all the magazines and books you can get your hands on. BUT DON'T TRADE YET.

The market will still be there when you complete your education. There is always another trade. But, if you trade too soon you run the risk of losing all your speculating capital and not being able to trade after your education is complete.

While you are a Phase One trader, you are like an infant learning to talk. You spend the first two years of your life listening. Likewise, spend the first phase of trading absorbing ideas. Listen to professional traders, attend seminars and workshops, but don't believe everything you hear. Absorb the information you are gathering and hold onto it, you'll be evaluating it in Phase Two.

During Phase One you should watch the market, but not enter any trades. Keep your charts, maintain your logs, even make paper trades if you wish. Keep your mind open to any and all possibilities, not forming any conclusions as yet about the nature of the market or the way you will trade it.

While you are in the investigation mode, begin to collect data and observe several markets. Market vehicles each have their own character. The rhythm of the market(s) you choose to trade must match your own for you to be successful trading it. Some people like to waltz, some prefer to fox-trot and still others enjoy the quickstep. This is a personal decision that only you can make and will require that you learn about each style before making your final choice.

For instance, if you trade individual stocks, you will hold trades longer than if you trade stock index futures. Remember, this job is about making money, and typically an individual stock will move fewer points during the day than will the stock index futures contract. A stock trader might

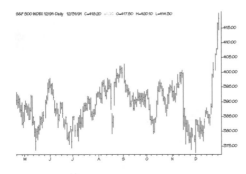

Figure 14.1   The S&P 500 futures contract often moves fast.

make several trades per year; a futures trader might make several trades per day. Only you can gauge your level of comfort with the pace of the trading vehicle. For instance, the S&P 500 futures contract often moves fast and with wide swings. Consider trading this vehicle if you have nerves of steel and no heart problems. (See Figure 14.1) For a slower moving vehicle note that bonds are related to interest rates and trend over long time periods. (See Figure 14.2)

When considering a trading vehicle, I always ask the question: **What's the potential hourly wage?** If in the 6.5 hours of a trading day you can expect to make $65 profit on average, then your wage is $10 per hour. If, on the other hand you trade a slow-moving instrument which will make you $65 per week, then in your 32.5 hour week you will make $2 per hour.

When measuring your potential dollar per hour wage, you need to measure how far that market moves per hour, and the likelihood of your catching that move. Before measuring the speed of markets, I put all charts on the same scale. You'll get a better idea of movement and rhythm if all charts are measured with the same ruler.

For instance, Figure 14.3 and 14.4 present two charts of IBM. The first chart is automatically scaled by the software.

I have scaled the second one manually so that the scale is 0 to 100. Visually you get a much different impression from these two charts.

I put all my charts on the same scale to make the PHW more evident.

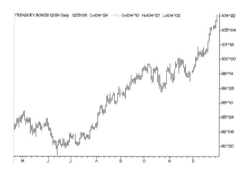

Figure 14.2   Bonds are related to interest rates and trend over long time periods.

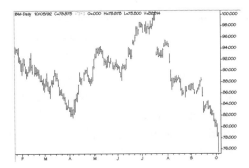

Figure 14.3 Chart of IBM automatically scaled by the computer

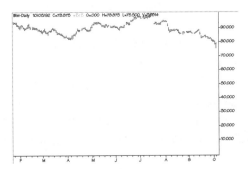

Figure 14.4 Chart of IBM manually scaled for PHW computation

Phase Two—Test

It's time to begin generating hypotheses and conducting experiments to either verify or disprove your hypotheses. The next chapter of this book will go into testing methods, but let's take a moment here for a brief overview.

Many technicians begin this stage with a preconceived notion and try to fit it to the market; I like to **start with the market** and try to find a notion that fits it. In Phase Two you are a researcher. Keep your lab notes as systematically as if you were a cancer researcher, remembering your high school biology techniques. It is appropriate to purchase one of

119

those bound, black and white marbled covered, lab books in which to keep notes. That way you can't cheat by tearing out pages and throwing them away.

In Chapter 4 and earlier in this chapter we started talking about the Potential Hourly Wage (PHW). This is such an important concept that we are going to talk about it again.

The first step in your testing agenda should be to determine whether any further pursuit of the trading vehicle in question is worth your time. Why go any further if it won't make you any money?

First, let's mark the obvious highs and lows on the chart in Figure 14.5. We'll use up-arrows to denote a low (from which the market moves up) and down-arrows to denote a high (from which the market moves down).

We don't know yet whether there's any money to be made here, we've just marked potential entry points and exit points.

Next we need to look at the scale of this chart to see whether the market movements between our entries and exits would be profitable. If, for instance, the time frame of this chart were a year and each move would only give us a couple of dollars profit, it's not worth our time.

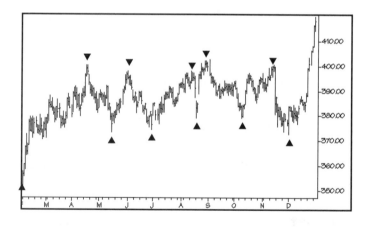

Figure 14.5   Mark the ideal entries and exits.

But, if it's a year and each move produces thousands of dollars, we'll go further with our analysis.

The scale on the right side of the chart shows that the data moves from 350 to 410, a 60 point move. This chart happens to be of the S&P 500 (my favorite trading vehicle), but it doesn't matter what we're observing, the test for fitness is the same. In the S&P 500, a move of one point is worth $500, so a move from 350 to 410 would be worth 60 * $500, or $30,000. The time frame in question is from February through December, a period of eleven months. Thirty thousand dollars in eleven months, that's $2,727 per month, or $16 per hour. That's our first rough approximation, but the answer is yes, this looks to be tradable.

Next we'll pretend that we could correctly catch each trade we've marked at the precise highs and lows. We'll calculate each trade's profit or loss and see what hourly wage could have been produced. The trades are displayed in the following table:

trade nbr	type	date	entry	date	exit	profit/loss
1	buy	1-Feb	350	25-Apr	400	$25,000
2	sell	25-Apr	400	10-May	375	$12,500
3	buy	10-May	375	1-Jun	400	$12,500
4	sell	1-Jun	400	1-Jul	375	$12,500
5	buy	1-Jul	375	12-Aug	400	$12,500
6	sell	12-Aug	400	16-Aug	380	$10,000
7	buy	16-Aug	380	1-Sep	400	$10,000
8	sell	1-Sep	400	10-Oct	380	$10,000
9	buy	10-Oct	380	4-Nov	400	$10,000
10	sell	4-Nov	400	1-Dec	375	$12,500
11	buy	1-Dec	375	31-Dec	415	$20,000
					TOTAL	$147,500

This type of trading system is called a **reversal system**, because each trade closes one position and opens another. You are always in the market, either long or short. Note that we have used closing prices for all the trades. The assumption here is that we have bought or sold the market at the closing price of the day, not any of the intra-day prices.

121

Calculating our PHW, we find that $147,500 in eleven months is $13,400 per month, or $80 per hour. That's respectable.

Now for a moment of truth. Before we can go any further we must take a second look at our pretense of catching each market move at the top and the bottom. That'll never happen. As a rule of thumb, I make the assumption that a good system can catch 60 percent of each market move. That's pretty realistic. With this in mind, 60 percent of $147,500 is $88,500, which is $48.27 per hour. Still respectable. Using 2,000 hours per year as a quick estimate, that gives us $96,545 per year trading one contract.

I call this part of the data analysis the "potential hourly wage analysis," or PHW. Before jumping into the numerical or pattern analysis phase, it's important to conduct these calculations. If the hourly wage is not acceptable, why would you want to spend time conducting all the remaining research?

We'll go into more depth about Phase II in the next chapter.

Phase Three—Follow Your System

Everything you do in developing your system presupposes that you will follow it. If you're not going to follow it, why spend the time researching it? Or why spend the money buying it?

Every successful trader will agree: if you are not disciplined enough to follow the rules you've set up, you will never be successful as a trader.

Disciplined trading is like flying an airplane on instruments. You train and train on your instruments so that when you get in a precarious situation you'll have an appropriate, automatic response. (Gas is right, brake is left.) When you get in the middle of the clouds and can't see anything, you certainly don't want to override your instruments! Your fear reaction could lead you straight into a mountain. In your trading your drawdown periods are the clouds. You don't know when you'll come out on the other side, and it's frightening. In spite of the fear, FOLLOW YOUR SYSTEM.

If you are having trouble following your system it could be one or more of several reasons. The first reason for not following a system is that you're not sure it works. If you haven't tested the system thoroughly through back-testing and forward-testing techniques, you won't trust it. And you shouldn't!

Secondary reasons for lacking discipline are often psychologically related and can be addressed by a trader's coach or trader's psychologist. Chapter 17 addresses some of these issues.

15 DEVELOPING YOUR OWN TRADING SYSTEM

Introduction

It is important to be the creator of your own trading methodology because it will be designed after your personality, your willingness to accept loss and, in your own time frame.

You may like to trade every day, or you might be a long-term trader, preferring to trade on a weekly or monthly basis. You might be the kind of individual who is willing to accept a large amount of risk in order to generate large gains, or you might be only willing to risk small amounts and accept small returns as a consequence. For these reasons, you should be the designer of your own trading methods.

The most difficult part of trading is discipline. If you have designed your own system and thoroughly tested it, you will have far more luck following it than if you are attempting to follow someone else's methodology.

System Design

Developing a trading system is 10 percent inspiration and 90 percent perspiration. It's like any scientific experiment, you come up with a theory and then run experiments to try and prove or disprove the theory.

In the very early days of my trading, I noticed that if the market has been going up during the last hour of trading and in the last five minutes it moves away from that trend and goes downward, that the open of the next day will gap up. I asked prominent traders and educators how many data points it took to prove a theory, and they all seemed to believe that 30 was sufficient.

With pen and paper (and a calculator) I tested this idea over the previous thirty days. It did great: 85 percent of the time the market responded as I had noticed! This was surely a money making prospect. So, the very next day I put my money in the market, using this newfound system, and lost. I tried it again the next day, and the day after. And lost.

What was wrong? I thought I had tested enough for this to be a proven system. Back to the drawing board, I worked backward for another thirty days, and found the system had only 30 percent success during that time period. It was then that I decided to investigate the possibility of testing concepts by computer and purchased *SystemWriter* (by Omega Research). I quickly found that this new theory of mine was only valid in the time frame in which I had observed it. Time to discard that idea and move on. In no time flat I had designed and tested dozens of systems, finding a few that worked and a lot that didn't. The value of software is that one can test many more theories much faster than with a calculator. The drawback is that there is a tendency to mistake force with power. You cannot force the computer to blast out a theory for you. You must use the power of your imagination and creativity to observe and theorize.

System design is a matter of noticing patterns, whether the patterns are chart patterns or numerical patterns or patterns involving days of the week. Pattern recognition was involved when A. Nonymous came up with the sayings:

Buy the rumor, sell the news. and
Buy the new moon, sell the full moon.

Or was it sell the new moon?

System design means looking at the following set of numbers and seeing a predictable pattern:

1 2 4 8 16 32 64
Clearly the next number in sequence should be 128.

How about this sequence:

1 1 2 3 5 8

This is the well known Fibonacci sequence which is generated by adding two adjacent numbers to form the next number. Therefore, the next number in this sequence would be 5+8, which is 13.

How about this more complex pattern:

1 11 21 1211 111221

If you can notice patterns to number sequences you can also see them in charts, whether they be bar charts, line charts, candle or volume charts.

Once you spot what you think is a pattern, then you must prove or disprove your theory.

Testing Your System

Without thorough testing, you will find yourself skeptical and doubtful. You will wonder whether your system has quit working. You will find that you are fearful of accumulating losses, because you have no way of knowing when the drawdown period should end.

Do not trade any system which has not been thoroughly tested and confirmed. If you do, you're not trading to make money, you're trading for the thrill.

As a mathematician and programmer, my view of the world is based in symbolic logic, and IF ... THEN statements. I'm a strong believer in cause and effect. Thus, as a trader, I view the markets in a systematic fashion, with mathematical definition. Decision trees (IF this happens,

THEN will follow, but IF the other happens, THEN something else will follow) rooted in mathematics are the basis for my trading.

Some may say that they trade on intuition, and that is their skill. My premise is that intuition is based on an unconscious set of rules, and that those rules can be translated to a computer program. Those who already trade with a set of clearly defined rules can immediately translate them to a computer program.

IF it's skill which generates the profits, THEN, consciously or unconsciously, the trader has a set of rules in mind. IF the trade is following rules, THEN the system can be tested and verified.

I have met many traders who test their rules by hand, that is, with paper and pencil and sometimes a calculator. There is nothing wrong with this method except that it is very time consuming, and the tendency to give up after testing only a small subset of the data is great. Further, I find the hand testing method to be prone to two types of error: wishful thinking and calculation error. Calculation error is obvious, one makes a simple arithmetic mistake. Wishful thinking goes like this: "Oh, I would have taken that trade, even though this system doesn't show it." It's akin to outsmarting the system, but is more subtle.

Another frequently used method of testing one's system is through the use of a spreadsheet, such as Lotus 1-2-3 or Excel. In the beginning of my trading experience, that is exactly what I did. And in fact, I still use spreadsheets to verify the accuracy of test results from other computer programs. The limitation with the spreadsheet method of testing is the amount of data a spreadsheet will handle, and the convenience and clarity of the output.

I am adamant about testing systems. Computer testing of systems is much like running a scientific experiment. Hypotheses are generated, assumptions are made, and the experiment is set up so as not to prejudice the results with the bias of the tester.

You may consider a trading system valid **only** after rigorous computer testing and verification. It must be tested over the largest set of data available. There is much discussion in the trading community about statistics: how many trades does it take to be statistically valid? The answer I have heard most often is "thirty." I couldn't disagree more.

My master's thesis was devoted to the subject of curve-fitting, that is, approximating a set of data with an equation, or curve. Having spent years in pursuit of just the right equation to approximate the data, I also know how to avoid curve-fitting. In the futures market, to fit the historical data accurately with a polynomial equation is to restrict the degrees of freedom to the extent that the future action will not be correctly predicted. In other words, the less complicated the model, the more it seems to work over time.

To test a system over a set of data which produces only thirty trades would generate a very nice model which would work well in the past, but as the markets fluctuate and the mood changes from bull, to bear, to sideways and back again, the model with thirty trades would probably prove to be only accurate over the subset of data you used for testing.

IF a system passes historical testing criteria and produces favorable results, THEN it must be traded without variation. IF the trader's testing is adequate, THEN the key to success is to hang in there. Do not give up during periods of drawdown.

Definition:

Drawdown
The reduction in account equity as a result of a trade or series of trades. (See Figure 15.1)

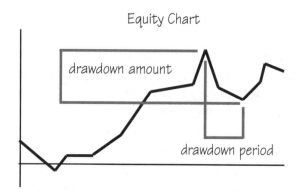

Figure 15.1 Equity chart showing period of drawdown.

Drawdown is an inevitable part of trading. Computer testing allows the most complete and accurate analysis of market data: Use it!

Computer trading is very similar to flying by instruments in an airplane. First you test your instruments, and then you test them again, THEN you must rely on those instruments and follow your flight plan without regard to the fog around you. The same is true with computerized trading. Establish your system, test it, test it again, and then trust your instruments. Trading then becomes as easy as 1,2,3.

Factoring In Costs

It's easy to pretend that we're trading in an ideal, computer model perfect environment while we're testing a new system. It makes all the numbers look better. Without any costs our profit is higher and our drawdown is lower. But this isn't the way it's going to behave in the real world where we are going to be trading.

To test your system under realistic conditions, you must include at least the two major costs to any trade: commission and slippage.

Definitions:

Commission:
The amount of money paid to a broker for a transaction.

Slippage:
The difference between the anticipated cost and the actual cost of a transaction.

Commission is negotiable. It is determined largely by how good a customer you are perceived as being. If you trade a large account frequently you can negotiate a lower commission than if you trade a small account infrequently. We have a full list of all the major brokerage firms both in *TC&RG* and on the Internet at *The Money Mentor*. Don't hesitate to call them asking for an information package and their rate structure. Shop around. Again, make a grid for your decision tree. Call as many brokerage houses as you can and make your decision only when you are fully informed.

Slippage is variable, and you will only determine this number after you've made a large number of trades with the broker you've chosen. Slippage happens with every middleman step. You see the trade on your computer, it takes a few seconds for you to call the broker on the telephone, he calls the trading desk, they call the trading floor, the floor broker signals the pit, and then the trade is filled. Every step takes time. During that time, trades are being rapidly transacted on the trading floor, changing the price of the instrument you wanted to buy or sell. So that you will have a fair idea of how much slippage to factor into your trading models and subsequent system testing, keep another spreadsheet (or add two columns to the one you already use). This time, keep track of the price at which your system told you to trade and the price at which your order was actually filled. After you've placed 20 or so trades with the broker in question, the average slippage of these trades can be used with fair confidence to represent slippage in your testing.

Slippage is not the same for all trading vehicles, so I can't give you a rule of thumb here. Stock trades will be entered with your broker and depending on the stock and its liquidity, your fill could vary dramatically from the price you wanted. In options trading the broker can tell you the bid and the ask, so you can have somewhat of an idea of the range your fill is likely to fall in. With futures trading, in liquid markets, the market moves quickly and you might enter an order to buy at 400 and get filled at 401. Anything's possible, and it not only depends on your broker, but how fast the market is moving when you enter your trade. In my futures trading, I'm not happy with any slippage over 1 percent.

Optimization

Every system has certain constants. These constants can always be turned into variables and then optimized. The danger is that most systems created on past data get over-optimized, curve-fitted, to that past data, so that in hindsight the results look terrific. Yet in the real world tomorrow's optimal parameters are almost always not the same as yesterday's optimal parameters. The system that worked so well on past data falls apart in the real world.

Optimization is not the enemy - abuse of optimization is.
—Ralph Vince, Portfolio Management Formulas

Once you have determined that your system or methodology works, that is it generates a profit over time, you can further refine it through optimization techniques.

Definition:

Optimization
Finding the best or most favorable conditions or parameters.

For instance, if you find that a moving average crossover system is profitable with parameters of 12 and 24, your next question should be, what if the parameters were 13 and 24?

It is easy to see that refining the parameters of your system through optimization could be an enormously time consuming process. To be thorough, you should test every meaningful combination of numbers, or specifically each of the following pairs:

```
(2,1),              (3,1),  (4,1),   (5,1) ... (24,1)
(1,2),              (3,2),  (4,2),   (5,2) ... (24,2)
```

all the way to

```
(1,24),             (2,24), (3,24),  ...       (23,24)
```

That's a lot of testing. In fact, it would mean you need to run 529 tests (23*23). [Not 24*24 since each of the identities (1,1), (2,2), etc. don't crossover.] It is here that many traders balk, and decide to just "guess" that the system works and go on. Thorough testing is tedious and a very lengthy process. Its value, however, is that once you have completed the entire testing process you can trust your system.

Optimization has suffered much bad press as a result of recent advances in computer software for traders. Several software packages offer optimization routines, which simplify the testing process and allow you to run 529 tests at the click of your mouse. However, these same programs, in the hands of the wrong users, can be used to fit tight curves through trading results so that the system is over-fitted and will work only for a short and specific time frame.

To avoid over-optimizing, I always test my theories over three sets of data. When developing an idea, I work with the middle third of the available data. For instance, I keep tick data from the inception of the S&P 500 Index futures contract, which began in April 1982. With twelve years of data I would use the period 1986—1989 for development. After, finding a theory that works in that time frame, I would back-test using the data from the period 1982—1985 and forward-test using the period 1990—1993. In the back- and forward-tests I do not change <u>any</u> of the parameters discovered in developing the theory. That would be curve-fitting.

Definition:

Curve-Fitting
Developing complicated rules that map known conditions.

If you use the entire set of data for your analysis and construct rules that map onto this data to produce optimal profits, then you will be curve fitting. Chances are this system will not work in the future.

If the system has been tested by the method of thirds proves profitable, then I would consider it a valid candidate for statistical analysis and money management techniques.

Money Management Techniques

Any system or trading methodology that works can be improved through proper money management techniques. As with everything else in this business, that's easy to say, now what does "works" mean?

"Works" means simply that over a long period of time the system can be expected to make a profit. In gambling casinos, the house has a small edge; over time the house will make a profit. But, it's a small edge, like 1-2 percent. That's all we really need in trading: a small edge. If we can be assured by mathematical and statistical means that our system has an edge, then we can use money management and discipline to provide consistently profitable results.

My favorite books on the subject of money management are written by the creative genius Ralph Vince. (Ralph was once a programmer for Larry Williams.) A descendant of Leonardo da Vinci (Ralph's immigrant grandfather Americanized the last name), Ralph carefully explains the theories underlying the topics and states definitively:

> . . . of the two, systems and money management, the money management is far and away more important in terms of your performance as a trader or fund manager.

He also notes, however, that

> Money management is predicated upon having a winning system.

I am so inspired by Ralph Vince's work that I once authored a twelve-page booklet called *Ralph Vince at a Glance*, which summarizes the concepts found in his book *Portfolio Management Formulas*. Ralph's original mathematical constructs are sometimes hard to follow, but boil down to a few pertinent equations and rules.

Basically, Ralph is saying that if you have a system which works (has a positive mathematical expectation) that you can dramatically improve its profit potential by appropriately varying the number of contracts you trade. There is a critical point on the curve generated by testing for the optimal number of contracts to trade, which if you exceed that number will surely lead to financial ruin (and quickly at that). But, if you stay on the left side of the curve, you can maximize your system's return. Ralph calls the fixed fraction divisor which maximizes return "optimal-f."

While it is true that the use of optimal-f maximizes your return, it is also true that it maximizes your risk. Ralph states "...the greater the return (up to but not beyond the optimal-f) the greater the risk."

I have found in my own research and use of optimal-f that it is important not to use this number as a fixed constant. To properly utilize the theory, optimal-f must be recomputed following the completion of each trade. Nevertheless, use of optimal-f requires the utmost discipline, as it increases drawdown in proportion to the return. (If you can't stand the heat, don't play with this fire.)

In his book *Money Management Strategies for Futures Traders*, Nauzer J. Balsara defines the percentage of capital to risk in trading thus:

$$\frac{[(A+1)p]-1}{A}$$

where A is the average payoff ratio and p is the average probability of success.

With this equation, and the statistical results of your system testing you can properly allocate your funds based on the profitability of your system.

For example, let's say you've done your homework and developed a system which is profitable 55 percent of the time and the average winning trade is $300, while the average losing trade is $100.

Your expected reward can be calculated as follows:

Expected Reward =
[% Winners * Avg $ Win] - [% Losers *Avg $ Loss]
or   [55% * $300] - [45%*$100]
     = $165 - $45
     = $120.

Now solving for A,

$$
\begin{aligned}
\left[\,(A+1)\,p - 1\right] &= 120 \\
\left[(A+1)(.55) - 1\right] &= 120 \\
.55A + .55 - 1 &= 120 \\
.55A - .45 &= 120 \\
.55A &= 119.5
\end{aligned}
$$

Therefore, $A = 217.27.$

Using this information in the equation for the optimal exposure fraction:

$$
\begin{aligned}
f &= \left[\,(217.27 + 1)\,.55 - 1\right] / 217.27 \\
&= 119.05 / 217.27 \\
&= 55\%
\end{aligned}
$$

Hence, you could risk 55 percent of your current bankroll on this trade.

Balsara goes further, to discuss allocating capital across multiple commodities which also lends itself to allocating capital across multiple systems. Use of either method is a form of diversification.

Both of these books are essential reading BEFORE you begin to trade. As stated earlier, money management is the key to the game. Any system with a positive mathematical expectation can be improved through money management techniques.

16 SETTING UP YOUR TRADING AS A BUSINESS

Developing Your Business Plan

Don't forget that you are running a business. Trading is not a hobby or a game. Starting with a book like *How to Prepare and Present a Business Plan* by Joseph R. Mancuso as a guide, develop a plan for your trading business as if you were going to present it to a finance committee. You must address not only the hope you have for enormous and instant profits, but the expenses you will immediately incur. It takes many years of planning and doing to become an overnight success.

In your business plan, you must consider at least the following costs:

- Brokerage Fees
- Computers
- Data
- Margin Requirements
- Office Supplies
- Software
- Telephone

After determining your fixed expenses, you can dream for a moment about how much profit you'll make. Then settle down to reality and factor in the results your system testing predicts for profits. Do not exaggerate this number; if you do, you'll only set yourself up for disappointment and failure.

Construct a spreadsheet for your break-even analysis, or use accounting paper, or even put it on plain paper. No matter what the form, get it in writing!

Breakeven analysis means you determine how much money you must make to cover all your expenses. The point at which you breakeven is where your income exactly covers your expenses: you make no money and you lose no money.

It takes a pretty good trader to make enough money to cover the overhead expenses month after month. This is not a get-rich-quick business, even though most beginning traders want it to be. (See Figures 16.1 and 16.2)

In addition to estimates of your setup costs and monthly expenses, your business plan should also include components that address structure, organization, and motivation:

- Overall mission statement
- Business objective
- Goals
- Tasks you must complete to reach your goals
- The complete and definitive rules of your trading system
- Statistics and mathematical results of back- and forward-testing of your trading system
- Money management rules
- Contingency plans: everything that could go wrong and everything that could go right.

Selecting a Broker

There are many factors you'll need to consider when chosing a brokerage firm to clear your trades. As with all the other business decisions you make, create a decision tree diagram, and begin your research. Call each brokerage firm and ask questions. Request their literature. Enter your findings in the table. Only after your research is complete should you

END-OF-DAY TRADER		
	Computer	$3,000
	Software	$500
	Data Feed	$50
	Telephone	$200

Figure 16.1   Beginning epenses for an end-of-day trader.

REAL-TIME TRADER		
	Computer	$3,000
	Software	$2,000
	Data Feed	$200
	Telephone	$300

Figure 16.2   Beginning epenses for a real-time trader.

make your decision. If you are happy with your broker and can form a long-term relationship, your business will benefit, so take your time in making the decision.

Full-Service vs. Discount

A full-service broker offers a variety of services not available at a discount brokerage. The concept behind discount brokerage is that they can offer you lower commission fees because you are making your own trading decisions, and don't need advise. A full-service brokerage employs people who can make recommendations and give you advise, and they pay these people from your higher commissions. One is not better than the other; you are not limited in the stocks or commodities you can buy through a discounter. The main difference is whether or not you want to pay for advice.

Brokerage Commissions and Fees

Brokerage fees **are not** the most important components in your decision process. Don't get me wrong, they certainly are important, just not **the**

most important. If you negotiate a low commission structure and you get bad fills, you'll be much worse off than if you have average commissions and get good fills.

Definition:

Fill
An executed order; sometimes the term refers to the price at which an order is executed.

Time Delay & Slippage

Bad fills on your order can happen in several ways. Let's say that your account is with a discount brokerage house and that you call your orders in to their order desk. The person at the order desk writes down the order and all relevant information and calls the broker on the floor of the exchange. The floor broker writes down the information and hand signals the information to the person in the pit. The guy in the pit stands there waving the hand signal for that order until someone else in the pit takes that bid or offer. The executed trade is hand-signaled back to the floor broker who calls the order desk who calls you back with the fill. All of that took time. During that passage of time there were other people buying and selling, which may have made prices move up or down from where they were when you first made the phone call. The difference between the price you wanted and the price you got is called **slippage**.

Electronic Trading

One way to reduce slippage, theoretically at least, would be through the use of electronic trading. At present this is not a reality in the U.S., although it is widely used in other countries. We do allow electronic trading through Globex in the overnight markets, but in our regular day markets we still use the open-outcry auction method. Theoretically speaking, if we entered our trading orders through our computers directly to the computers at the exchange, the transaction would take place almost instantaneously, eliminating slippage and time delays.

Setting Up Your Account

Once you've completed your research into brokerage commissions you will ask the brokeage firm you've chosen to send you all the necessary forms for opening a new account. Fill them out carefully, keep a copy for yourself, and send them back to the broker with your deposit to open the account. When they've established the account, usually just a few days, they'll call you back with an account number and a phone number to call to make your trades.

The amount of your opening deposit will be governed by the level at which you will be trading. For instance, if you are going to be trading stocks in lots of 100, and the stocks on average cost $50 per share, the minimum you should put in the account would be $5,000. However, if your first trade is a loss (and Murphy's law says it should be) you will immediately need to put more money in the account to cover the loss. As a rule of thumb, I put twice the required minimum in the account. In this case then, you would put $10,000 in the account. In the case of futures trading, where you are highly leveraged you should open the account with twice the required margin.

Margin Requirements

Definition:

Margin
In stock trading, an account in which purchase of stock may be financed with borrowed money; in futures trading, the deposit placed with the clearing house to assure fulfillment of the contract. This amount varies with market volatility and is settled in cash.

In practice, stocks can typically be purchased on 50 percent margin. If you want to purchase $10,000 worth of stock you can do it with $5,000 cash. The requirements for you to do this vary with brokerage houses, so check with your broker first.

Margin requirements for futures contracts varies with the volatility of the market and also differs among commodities. Around 1985, the margin for the S&P 500 futures contract was $6,500. By October 1987 the margin had increased to $22,000 per contract. Now, in 1995, the margin for the same contract is at $12,000.

Entering Your First Trade

Your first trade is probably the most scary trade you'll ever enter. After you've spent months in research and paper-trading, you'll be eager to make that first trade, but if you're like me you'll be very nervous about it. As I approached that time, I remember having visions of grade school kids on the playground jumping rope. It felt like that moment when the rope is turning, you're standing there watching it, getting the rhythm right, but you're afraid you might fall if you jump in.

The key things you need to remember when placing this first order are:

- follow your system
- speak clearly and distinctly
- tell the person on the other end of the phone only what they need to know to place your order (they usually don't want to chat)

A typical order will sound something like this: Sunny Harris, account 1234, buy 100 shares IBM market.

The long way of saying this would be: Hi. This is Sunny Harris. My account number is 1234. I would like to buy 100 shares of IBM at the current market price.

Order Types

You may enter other types of orders than market orders. In fact, there are many types of orders, but not all markets accept all type of orders. Ask your broker what types of orders they accept.

For your reference, here's a list of order types:

cancel	cancel and replace	disregard tape (DRT)
limit	limit on close	market
market if touched (MIT)	market on close (MOC)	market on open only
or better close only	order cancels order	spread
stop	stop close only	stop limit
stop limit close only	stop with limit of _____	

These terms don't always mean the same thing in different settings. Your broker can tell you which order types they accept and give you the meanings of the terms they accept.

Legal and Tax Questions

Don't invest or trade for the tax man. By that I mean, if you consider the tax consequences of a transaction before you consider the profit potential and risk-reward ratio, then you're investing for the tax man. Taxes don't matter. Would you rather make 10 percent tax-free on an investment—or 100 percent and have to pay taxes?

The more money you make the more taxes you get to pay. That's a good thing. It just means you're making more money.

Consult with your tax accountant or tax attorney about your individual situation.

Lawyers

You may or may not need an attorney before you start trading. Only you will know that. If you are trading only for your own account, and do not take money from anyone else, chances are you don't need an attorney for your trading. If, on the other hand, you are considering managing money for friends or clients, you definitely will need an attorney. Legal advise is well beyond the scope of this book and our expertise. If you think there is any reason you might need an attorney, consult the one(s) you already employ or take a look in the yellow pages of *TC&RG* and start calling around.

Books

There's not a lot written about the business aspects of trading. The one book which comes to mind is *Trading is a Business* by Joe Ross. Beyond that, general business management books and business planning books will help point you in the right direction.

Regulators

Again, if you trade only for your own account, you probably don't need to worry about regulators. Regulators are there to protect the unsuspecting public from you. If you begin advertising your successes and inviting the public to let you manage their money, then you will be subject to the regulations of the organization which oversees the type of trading you will be doing. There are regulators for futures trading, options trading, stock trading, etc.

Here are some of the numbers you'll need to call. Ask for their literature and information about their regulations, so you'll be safe and not sorry.

- Commodity Futures Trading Commission   1-202-254-8630
- NASDAQ, Inc.   1-202-728-8000
- National Association of Securities Dealers   1-312-899-4400
- National Futures Association   1-312-781-1372
- Securities & Exchange Commission   1-202-942-0020

17 DISCIPLINE

Introduction

I am a mathematician, not a psychologist. For this reason I asked one of the prominent traders' coaches to pen much of this chapter. Adrienne Laris Toghraie, of *Trading on Target*, was kind enough to donate her insight and experience to this effort.

Following Your System

Every successful trader will agree: **If you are not disciplined enough to follow the rules you've set up, you will never be successful as a trader.**

However, discipline is not a character trait you can wish into existence just because you want to be successful. To be disciplined, you must possess three key psychological elements:

1. Motivation
2. Commitment
3. Persistence

Developing these traits is an ongoing process for most of us. We attend motivational seminars; we take classes; we go to trade shows and retreats; all to hone our skills and replenish our psychological strengths. Trading is a constant process of education and research.

Motivation

You must be driven by passion in order to overcome the procrastination that most people feel when beginning any new venture. Passion is an intensity of feeling that narrows your focus and consolidates your energy toward a single goal.

Passion is the energy that propels you into immediate action. The same level of dedication and energy which is required to become a surgeon, a lawyer, or an astronaut is required to become a professional trader.

Every individual is motivated by a unique set of triggers. What works for one person may not work for another. For that reason, research in the field of personal motivation has demonstrated that you already have all it takes: you do not need someone else to do it for you. To recognize your own motivational model, remember the times in your life when you completed a difficult task or reached a goal because you were passionately motivated. Having identified these past successful achievements, model your current behavior accordingly.

Modeling simply means copying success. To create high achievement for yourself, model your actions after your own previous successes or the successes of others.

Commitment

All achievement requires commitment. The bigger the goal, the higher the level of commitment required. A commitment is a promise you make to yourself. When you have the goal of becoming a trader, each task you complete towards that goal builds trust. When commitments are broken, the unconscious mind will not support us in keeping our agreements. Therefore, it is essential to build a pattern of trust between you and yourself when you are in the development stage. You build this trust pattern by completing each task within your agreed time frame.

A strategy for learning how to keep commitments is to set small achievable tasks and complete them. This gives a pattern of biological feedback for your neurology to follow. Attaching a small reward that makes you feel good is an excellent way to anchor task achievement. Several task achievements in a row will lead to a goal achievement. This positive pattern is the foundation necessary to follow your own rules. This, in-and-of-itself, is a major accomplishment for all traders and is the basis for success.

Most people make commitments before they understand the trade-offs attached to those commitments. It takes sacrifice, investment of time, resources and psychological challenges to become a professional trader. Sacrifice does not mean neglecting everything and everyone else in your life, however. You must balance all areas of your life, or you will create a breeding ground for self-sabotage. Self-sabotage is the worst trap a trader (or anyone else) can fall into, because those who fall sometimes never recover.

Persistence

Studying to be a trader can be a very lonely process. Many traders feel they are not a trader until they actually put on that first trade. It is important for your motivation to have the attitude that you are a trader once you have made the commitment, and that each step is an important part of the process for success. When you choose the right actions in the developmental stage, you will eliminate many of the psychological struggles traders go through when they begin to trade.

It is essential that you not give up too early. Persistence means "continuing in the face of opposition." For every good idea you have, which actually profits in the market, you will have 99 ideas which fail. It is the persistence which differentiates long-term successful traders from the other 80 percent who give up.

Keeping a Diary

It is essential for you as a trader to know your daily, weekly and monthly achievements. Maintaining a log of your accomplishments will document the progress you have made. This is important so that you can celebrate your progress, rather than falling into the mind-trap that little has been accomplished.

It is also important that you keep a careful and precise diary of events in the market, so that you can later form conclusions from the data. To this day, Joe Granville keeps a daily diary of trading!

From your diary you can infer that certain types of economic reports generate fear and therefore down days in the market. You can conclude that the market has specific characteristics at specific times of day. You can analyze the behavior of your system from your diary, as well.

What's Between You and Following Your Rules?

There are many psychological pitfalls you can face when you start to trade your system. Trading is the performance of all the best and worst parts of your psychology. Some of the psychological challenges that traders must conquer when trying to follow their systems are:

1. Emotions
2. Conflicts
3. Attitudes
4. Beliefs

Emotions

Fear is the major emotion that holds most traders back. You must have preparedness in your trading plan. Then you must satisfy the needs of the part of you that is afraid to take the correct trading actions, for example, if you are afraid to enter the markets, perhaps you should have someone else initiate the trade.

Conflicts

First, you must recognize the conflicts you have within yourself, i.e. part of you is afraid to take risk, and part of you knows it should stick to your money management rules. Negotiate between these two parts of yourself to come up with an amicable working relationship.

Attitudes

Reframe your negative attitudes! A common negative attitude shared by traders is "it is a losing day if I lose money." Transform this negative attitude thus: "It is a losing day only if I do not follow my system and learn the lessons the market is teaching me." All traders experience drawdown. It is part of doing business.

Beliefs

Your beliefs are what is true for you. It is important to notice what you believe about yourself as a successful trader, what you believe about your system, and what you believe about making money. Beliefs direct our neurology to the kind of action that manifests our getting what we believe in. ("Be careful what you ask for, you might get it.")

If you have negative beliefs about becoming a successful trader, change this by beginning to dwell upon what positive beliefs would be more resourceful, until they stir you into positive feelings. ("What you think about, you bring about.") For instance, if you are thinking, "I can never be a top trader," transform your thoughts to "If I do all the things a top trader does, I will be a top trader."

Coaches and Psychologists

The foregoing is a brief overview (by Adrienne Toghraie, of Trading on Target) of some of the psychological challenges that can face you as a trader. Entire books are devoted to these subjects, specifically for traders. Seminars and workshops focus on the psychology of trading.

Accomplished traders all agree that conquering the psychological aspects makes all the difference in attaining positive trading results.

This is easier said than done. While you cannot have trust and discipline without a proven trading system or methodology, the best system in the world will do you no good without the discipline to follow it. These two elements go hand-in-hand.

You don't hesitate to take golf lessons or dance lessons or classes about someone's system of trading—so don't hesitate to take lessons on the psychological aspects of trading. Professional help can save you from running into considerable unnecessary losses. All you have to do is monitor your performance, be honest with yourself and take the right actions.

Who You Gonna Call?

Coaches and psychologists who deal specifically with the financial community do more than counsel you through difficult emotional times. These specialists offer motivational training, cassette tapes, video tapes, literature and seminars in addition to telephone and personal consulting

Charles Faulkner
Mental Edge Trading Associates
141 W Jackson Dr Ste 278
Chicago, IL 60604
1-800-500-7657 fax 1-800-500-7657

Dr. Richard McCall
Misogi International
PO Box 23413
Little Rock, AR 72221
1-800-336-7061 fax 1-501-568-8157

Adrienne Toghraie
Trading on Target
100 Lavewood Lane
Cary, NC 27511
1-919-851-8288 fax 1-919-851-9979

Van K. Tharp
Van Tharp Associates
8308 Belgium St
Raleigh, NC 27606
1-919-362-5591 fax 1-919-362-6020

18 EVALUATING YOUR PERFORMANCE

Introduction

At the very least, you must know the profit or loss of each trade you make. Keeping a running total of your profits and losses keeps you honest. Gamblers talk about their big wins, but they never tell you about their losses. Trading is not gambling, it is a profession, so keep good books.

For every trade you make, you must record the price at which you entered the trade and the price at which you exit. From these two numbers you compute your profit or loss.

Definition:

Profit
The difference between the price at which you sell something and the price at which you bought it, less any transaction costs.

If your trade was long, that is you bought and then sold in that order, then your profit is calculated as:

$$\text{Profit} = \text{Exit Price} - \text{Entry Price}$$

If your trade was short, that is you sold and then bought in that order, then your profit is calculated as:

$$\text{Profit} = \text{Entry Price} - \text{Exit Price}$$

I cannot stress to you strongly enough: **keep good books**. I don't care whether you use plain white paper and a pen, or green ledger paper or a computer, but keep track of everything you do. Otherwise, you're just gambling and you have no statistics upon which to base subsequent calculations which can improve your performance.

See Figure 18.1 for an example of keeping track of your trades in a spreadsheet. This is the very **least** you must know. But's it is not really enough. We math types call this "necessary, but not sufficient." You can keep better statistics than these, and thereby have more confidence in your trading.

Your **equity** is the cumulative amount of money you have made or lost trading. In the spreadsheet above, the equity is in column G, and is calculated by adding all your profits and subtracting all your losses.

The more you know about your trading statistically, the more able you will be to follow it during periods of drawdown. (See Figure 18.2)

Definition:

Drawdown
The reduction in account equity as a result of a losing trade or series of losing trades.

	A	B	C	D	E	F	G
1	Date	Time	Type	Cts	Price	Entry P/L	Cumulative
2	10/10/95	12:45 PM	Buy	1	$580.70		
3	10/11/95	12:55 PM	LExit	1	$582.65	$945.00	$945.00
4	10/13/95	11:00 AM	Sell	1	$590.40		
5	10/17/95	9:45 AM	SExit	1	$586.50	$1,920.00	$2,865.00

Figure 18.1 Keeping your trades in a spreadsheet.

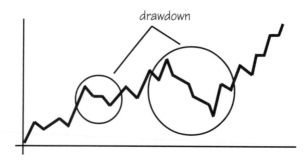

drawdown

Figure 18.2 *An equity chart showing periods of drawdown.*

In practice, we measure drawdown from the highest equity high to the lowest equity low. Looking at this number answers the question: "How bad can it be?" What's your worst case?

Useful Statistics

In addition to keeping track of your equity and your drawdown, there are several other numbers you should compute. Many of the financial software products will calculate these statistics automatically for you as part of their portfolio modules.

Figure 18.3 gives an example of the information available from a Performance Summary from TradeStation™ (Omega Research).

Study the information in Figure 18.3. There's a lot to be learned. The total net profit is not the most important number. We know from Chapter 15 that if the system is profitable (has a positive mathematical expectation) we can maximize the profit through money management; so as long as the total net profit is positive, we can improve it.

The first thing I look at in this figure is the **largest winning trade**. If the largest winning trade accounts for most of the profit, then the system probably won't continue to work over time. I like to see profits accumulate a little bit at a time, which shows me that the system wins in a variety of market environments.

Secondly, I look at the **number of trades** and the size of the **average trade**. With 20 trades we know we have made enough trades to begin evaluating the system's behavior (as opposed to 2 or 3 trades). We know

```
Performance Summary: All Trades
Total net profit          $ 6,275    Open position P/L          $ 2,425
Gross profit              $13,720    Gross loss                 $ -7,445

Total # of trades             20    Percent profitable            55%
Number winning trades         11    Number losing trades            9

Largest winning trade     $ 2,870    Largest losing trade       $ -2,255
Average winning trade       $1,247   Average losing trade       $ -827
Ratio avg win/avg loss       1.51    Avg trade (win & loss)      $314

Max consec. winners           5    Max consec. losers              3
Avg # bars in winners        26    Avg # bars in losers            8

Max intraday drawdown     $ -3,315
Profit factor                1.84    Max # contracts held            1
Account size required     $ 15,315   Return on account             41%
```

Figure 18.3 Performance Summary.

from the size of the average trade that we're making enough money to get in and out of the trade and account for slippage and the time it takes to actually enter the trade in the market.

Professional traders can make a good living with systems which show 40 percent or more profit as long as the **ratio of the average win to average loss** is high enough to generate a positive mathematical expectation. Since the figure above shows that 55 percent of the trades are profitable, that's acceptable. We calculate that number by taking the total number of winning trades (11) and dividing by the total number of trades (20).

Finally I look at the **maximum consecutive losers** and the average number of bars in losers to see whether my emotional makeup and personality can stand the heat in this kitchen. Looking at the figure again, there are 3 losers in a row before encountering a winning trade. That's not too bad emotionally. And there are only 8 bars, on average, in each losing trade while the winners, on average, last for 26 bars. I think I can handle that.

Other programs provide additional trade information like how many times your stop was hit, total commission expenses, maximum equity drop, maximum trade drawdown, margin interest expenses, interest earned and commission to equity ratio.

An important component of any trading software is the ability to display a chart of your equity. Since these programs are always graphically oriented, and a chart is worth a thousand numbers, it only makes sense to be able to visually inspect the progress of your trading.

The most powerful of system testing software, *Excalibur for Windows* by Futures Truth offers even more statistics about your trading results than those mentioned above. Included in its Summary Report are: Optimal-f, Pessimistic Return, Geometric Mean, Sharpe Ratio, Percent of Time in the Market and Longest Flat Time.

In addition to these statistics, *Excalibur* offers more extensive reports which assist in your total understanding of your system. Included are: Drawdown Report, Monthly Trade Breakdown, Day of Week Analysis, Time of Day Trade Breakdown, Composite Reports, Trade Detail Report, and Risk Reports.

There are other statistics which professional traders use to monitor the success (or failure) of their trading. When you get to that point, a good book to study is *Managed Futures in the Institutional Portfolio* by Charles B. Epstein, where you can find coverage of such topics as Standard Deviation, Sharpe Ratio, Sterling Ratio, Maximum Drawdown, Recovery Time, Risk and Risk of Ruin.

If you decide to diversify and trade more than one system, or more than one instrument (like stocks and sugar futures), then you need to know whether the systems are correlated. If two systems produce essentially the same results they are said to be highly correlated; if two systems are opposite each other (one wins when the other loses and vice versa) they are not correlated. Depending on the profitability of the systems, two non-correlated techniques could conceivably eliminate drawdown periods by covering for each other. One's winning while the other is losing.

If two systems are highly correlated, then would you trade them both? In that situation you would be winning twice as fast, but you'd also be losing twice as fast.

For these reasons, it is important to determine the correlation coefficient to multiple trading systems before you trade them together.

The formula and explanation of this procedure is also to be found in Chuck Epstein's book, mentioned above.

Ralph Vince covers valuable concepts in his books which are **musts** for the serious evaluation of your performance. Before you devote yourself to the religious following of your system, run your hypothetical trades through a few of Ralph's exercises. You'll either discard your system as unworkable or you will gain great insight into how to maximize your system's profits. The books by Vince to-date are: *The Mathematics of Money Management*, *Portfolio Management Formulas*, and *The New Money Management*.

19 BACK OFFICE DETAILS

Introduction

What the heck is a back office, you say! You don't even have a front office. Well, in trading terminology back-office means the stuff that goes on behind the scenes. Your system and the events of actually trading are front-office tasks. The paperwork part, where you keep track of each and every detail about your individual trades, their statistics, the account balance, your checking account, how much you spend on office supplies . . . that's back-office information.

If you are a small time operator, keeping your logs and running balance on a piece of grid paper or ledger paper may be good enough. When I first began trading, I kept these details in a spreadsheet.

As time goes on, and your profits grow, your business will naturally expand. At some point the spreadsheet method won't be enough. You will have so many trades and formulas in the spreadsheet that you start losing track of things. You'll find it difficult to produce the summary reports you will want. When that happens, you will want to consider using a software program designed for back office accounting, or you might consider using a professional accounting firm which specializes in back office accounting for traders.

Accounting

Do It Yourself?

Doing it yourself with an accounting program designed for traders presents two immediate advantages: you are in control of your documentation and you will gain insight into your system's successes and failures. Often the process of documenting your trades will cause you to think of ways to improve the results, as you begin to recognize patterns to your profits and losses.

Several companies offer back office accounting software for traders:

- Atis International, Inc.   1-312-527-2847
- Austin Associates   1-316-788-3255
- Brokerage Systems, Inc.   1-312-559-0250
- Commodity Systems, Inc.   1-800-274-4727
- Kokanee Systems Software, Inc.   1-800-661-4599
- Orbit Software   1-800-369-6398
- TradeManagement Systems, Inc.   1-708-323-5238
- TradeVision, Inc.   1-619-930-1050

To some extent you can even use accounting programs like *Quicken* to keep track of your trading, depending on what you are trading. Quicken can keep track of stocks, bonds, mutual funds, REITs and partnerships, IRAs or Keogh accounts, variable annuities, Money Market Funds, CDs or Treasury Bills, Real Estate, and Retirement Plans.

As with all your research, as you become interested in purchasing software to keep track of your trading, call each of the vendors, get their literature and demo disk, make a table of pros and cons and evaluate each package before making a purchase.

Accountants

In the computer database that I maintain for creating *TC&RG* and *The Money Mentor* I have hundreds of accountants listed who work with traders. I can't possibly list them all here, that's what my magazine is for. What you need to know is that there is such a list and that not all accountants are versed in the whys and wherefores of trading. Your income tax accountant is not necessarily the person who can administer your trading records. Specialized accountants stay on top of regulations that restrict and govern your trading, as well as being able to give you hints about some of the best strategies for minimizing your tax liability.

Back Office Services

Several firms offer a package of complete service which frees you from assuming the role of clerk and accountant and lets you focus on your trading methods. While these services are usually expensive, if you become a frequent or large trader (that's the goal isn't it?) you may need to engage one of these services. Again, I keep the list up-to-date in other media, but a few you might want to contact are:

- Acceltek Accounting Systems   1-312-804-0074
- Commodity Compliance Services, Inc. 1-800-445-6535
- Korr Accounting Systems   1-801-645-7288
- Organizer Systems, Inc.   1-201-262-1120
- Trade Management Systems, Inc.   1-708-323-5238

Legal and Tax Questions

Don't invest or trade for the tax man. By that I mean, if you consider the tax consequences of a transaction before you consider the profit potential and risk-reward ratio, then you're investing for the tax man. Taxes don't matter. Would you rather make 10 percent tax-free on an investment or 100 percent and have to pay taxes?

The more money you make the more taxes you get to pay. That's a good thing. It just means you're making more money.

Ted Tesser's *The Serious Investor's Tax Survival Guide* is the one book you need to read when it comes to this aspect of trading. Ted covers everything you need to know and watch out for, including deductions and expenses, passive versus investment income, audits, calculating your true investment return after taxes and "how far can we go".

The tax law with respect to capital gains, allowable expenses and tax rates changes frequently. Consult your attorney and your tax accountant for advice on these subjects.

Lawyers

Again the list is lengthy and not published in this book, but available in *TC&RG* or *The Money Mentor*. If you need a lawyer, be sure to get one who specializes not only in trading endeavors, but who specializes in the particular aspect of trading with which you need help. I think attorneys specialize in even narrower subspecialities than do physicians.

Regulators

Several organizations exist to protect the public from malpractice in the exchanges. Each of these regulating bodies has its own set of guidelines governing what you can and can't do. There are circumstances under which you can trade money for your friends and situations in which you can't. These restrictions change with time, so if you consider trading anyone's money besides your own, be sure to contact one or all of the agencies below.

CFTC—Commodity Futures Trading Commission

The CFTC was established by the Commodity Futures Trading Commissions Act of 1974, along with the NFA. An independent agency with exclusive jurisdiction over futures trading.

NFA—National Futures Association

NFA is a not-for-profit membership corporation formed in 1976 to become a futures industry's self-regulatory organization under Section 17 of the Commodity Exchange Act.

NASDAQ—National Association of Securities Dealers

An agency that represents securities dealers who trade for themselves in the U.S. It is empowered by the U.S. Securities and Exchange Commission to regulate dealers' operations in the over-the-counter markets, and has the authority to censure, fine, suspend, or expel members who break its rules.

SEC—Securities and Exchange Commission

An independent U.S. Federal regulatory agency, created by the Securities Exchange Act of 1934, that administers statutes designed to provide the fullest possible disclosure to the investing public and to protect the interest of both the general public and investors against malpractice in the securities and financial markets. The SEC supervises all national securities exchanges and associations, registers all issues of securities offered in the interstate commerce or through the mail, registers brokers and dealers who engage in over-the-counter trading, and regulated mutual funds and other investment companies, investment counselors and advisors, and practically all other individuals and firms engaged in the investment business.

20 CONCLUSION

There is possibly nothing more satisfying than working for yourself, generating your income your own way. There is also probably nothing more difficult and all consuming.

When you work for yourself, or own your own business, you have a "full-time" job—24 hours a day. There are no vacations, no sick days, and no one else to blame when things go wrong. But, you can wear shorts to work if you want to and come and go at your own pace.

Step by Step

I am often asked to provide a checklist for beginners, against which you can measure your progress. Most beginning traders don't want to hear what I am about to say, but come back to me after they are experienced, acknowledging that this admonition is indeed true.

There are three phases to becoming a successful trader:

Phase I—Acquiring Information

1. Listen to what others have to say, to the news, to forecasts, to lectures and seminars.
2. Observe the action of the market, observe patterns and results.
3. Read everything you can get your hands on.

Phase II—Developing Your System

1. Research
2. Test your theories with pen, paper and a calculator.

3. Test your theories in a spreadsheet.
4. Test your theories with analysis software.
5. If your theory merits further investigation, based on the first four steps, run exhaustive tests by thirds. (See chapter 15.)
6. Develop a system which has a **positive mathematical expectation**, which pays you an acceptable potential hourly wage, and with which you are comfortable.

Phase III - Following Your System

1. **Paper trade**. Without lying to yourself, put on paper (in ink, with time stamps) each and every trade your system calls for.
2. When you are confident that you can follow every signal your system gives, then you may begin to actually **enter trades** in the market.
3. Do not vary from the rules you have established! If you conclude that you must override your rules at some juncture, then you haven't properly tested and verified your rules. **Do not trade if you can't follow your system**. Go back to Phase II and conduct additional research until you have so thoroughly defined and exhaustively tested your rules that you can trade your system like flying on instruments.

Write me a note to let me know how you're doing.

I wish you success in direct proportion to your effort,

Sunny J. Harris

APPENDIX A—INTERNET SITES

American Stock Exchange	http://www.amex.com
Bank of America	http://www.bofa.com
Barra	http://www.barra.com
The Better Business Bureau	http://www.cbbb.org/cbbb
Biz Web	http://www.bizweb.com
Bloomberg Business News	http://www.bloomberg.com
Books of Wall Street	http://www.ambook.org/bookstore/fraser
Charles Schwab Online	http://www.schwab.com
Chicago Board of Trade	http://www.cbot.com
Chicago Board Options Exchange	http://www.cboe.com
Chicago Mercantile Exchange	http://www.cme.com
Corporate Financials Online	http://cfonews.com
Dreyfus Online Information Center	http://networth.galt.com/dreyfus/4134
Dun & Bradstreet Information Services	http://www.dbisna.com
ENews (Electronic Newsstands)	http://enews.com
E*Trade	http://www.etrade.com
Experimental Stock Market Data	http://www.ai.mit.edu/stocks
Fidelity Investments	http://www.fid-inv.com
FinanceNet	http://www.financenet.gov
First Chicago Capital Markets, Inc.	http://fccm.com
FINWeb	http://finweb.bus.utexas.edu/finecon
Futures and Options Trading Group	http://www.teleport.com/~futures

GNN NetNews	http://gnn.com/news/index
GNN Personal Finance Center	http://gnn.interpath.net/gnn/meta/finance
Investing Online	http://risc.cpbx.net/IOL/about
Ira Epstein Brokerage	http://www.iraepstein.com
MidAmerica Commodity Exchange	http://www.midam.com
The Money Mentor	http://www.moneymentor.com
Mortgage Strategies	http://www.ais.net/netmall/mortgage/mortgage
NetWorth	http:///networth.galt.com

New York Stock Exchange
http://www.cob.ohio-state.edu:80/~fin/resources_data/provider/nyse

Quote.Com	http://www.quote.com
Schwab Online	http://www.Schwab.Com/SchwabOnline
USA Today	http://alpha.acast.nova.edu/usatoday

APPENDIX B—MAGAZINES

Financial Trader $38/yr
PO Box 1177 • Skokie, IL 60076• (708) 647-4065

Financial World $37.50/yr
1328 Broadway • New York, NY 10001 • (212) 594-5030

Futures $39/yr.
219 Parkade • Cedar Falls, IA 50613 • (319) 277-1278

Futures & Options World $230/yr.
Park House • Park Terrace • Worchester Park, Surrey KT4 7HY UK

Institutional Investor $350/yr.
488 Madison Ave • New York NY 10022 • (800) 346-9759

Technical Analysis of Stocks and Commodities $64.95/yr.
4757 California Ave, SW • Seattle, WA 98116 • (206) 938-0570

Traders' Catalog & Resource Guide $99/yr.
2075 Corte del Nogal Ste C • Carlsbad, CA 92009 • (619) 930-1050

Traders World $15/yr
2508 Grayrock St • Springfield, MO 65810 • (417) 882-9697

Wall Street & Technology $85/yr.
PO Box 1054 • Skokie, IL 60076 • (708) 647-4065

APPENDIX C—NEWSPAPERS

Barrons

PO Box 300 • Princeton, NJ 08543 • (609) 520-4244

Investor's Business Daily

12655 Beatrice Ave • Los Angeles, CA 90056 • (310) 448-6600

USA Today

100 Wilson Blvd • Arlington, VA 22229 • (800) USA-0001

Wall Street Journal

WFC 200 Liberty St • New York, NY 10281 • (212) 416-4201

APPENDIX D—ON-LINE SERVICES

America On-Line

8619 Westwood Center Dr • Vienna, VA 22182 • (800) 827-6364

CompuServe

5000 Arlington Center Blvd • Columbus, OH 43220 • (614) 457-8600

e*World (Apple Computer Inc.)

20525 Mariani Ave • Cupertino, CA 95014 • (408) 996-1010

GEnie

401 N Washington St • Rockville, MD 20850 • (800) 638-9636

Microsoft Network

One Microsoft Way • Redmond, WA 98052 • (800) 426-9400

Prodigy

445 Hamilton Ave • White Plains, NY 10601 • (800) 776-3449

APPENDIX E—SOFTWARE VENDORS

AIQ, Inc.	Trading Expert, StockExpert, Market Expert	1-800-332-2999
Arms Equivolume	Equivolume Charting	1-800-223-2767
Bristol Financial Services	Insight Trading Software	1-714-240-0990
Brownstone Productions, Inc.	Altima	1-800-642-7116
Business Week & Morningstar	Business Week Mutual Scoreboard	1-800-553-3575
Center for Elliott Wave Analysis	Elliott Wave Analyser	011-61-9-457-0069
Commodity Systems, Inc.	QuickPlot/QuickStudy	1-800-274-4727
Dow Jones Dow Jones	Market Monitor	1-800-815-5100
Equis International	MetaStock, Technician	1-800-882-3040
Financial Information Management	Prophet	1-800-532-0136
Institute for Options Research	Option Master	1-800-334-0854 x840
Integrated Financial Solutions	Quote Express	1-800-729-5037
Investor's FastTrack	FastTrack	1-800-749-1348
Kasanjian Research	Nature's Pulse	1-909-337-0816
Linn Software	TickerWatcher (Macintosh)	1-800-546-6842
Manhattan Analytics, Inc.	Monocle	1-800-251-3863
Man Machine Interfaces Inc	Genetic Algorithm Software	1-800-367-4242
Mantic Software Corp	Options Laboratory	1-800-730-2919
MarketArts, Inc	Windows on Wall Street	1-800-998-VIEW
NIBS	NeuroForecaster	011-65-344-2357
Nirvana Systems, Inc.	Profit Tester	1-800-880-0338
NTech	Behold!	1-512-328-8000
Omega Research	SuperCharts & TradeStation	1-800-422-8587 x927c
Optionomics	Optionomic Systems	1-800-255-3374
OptionVue Systems Int'l	DataVue, OptionVue IV	1-800-733-6610
Orbit Software	Electric Scorecard II	1-800-369-6398
Papyrus Technology	Clarity & Composer	1-800-628-6435
RMC	MarketMaster	1-408-773-8715
Roberts-Slade	FirstAlert, ChartistAlert, RiskAlert, ...	1-800-433-4276
RTR Software Inc.	Technifilter Plus	1-919-510-0608
RW Systems	Trading Recipes	1-800-449-4828
Stratagem Software Int'l	SMARTrader	1-800-779-7353
Technical Tools	TT Chart Book	1-800-231-8005
Telescan, Inc.	Modelware, Mutual Fund Edge, Options ...	1-800-324-8246
Townsend Analytics, Ltd	Options Risk Mgt, Realtick III, TA-SRV	1-800-827-0141
TradeVision, Inc.	Abacus	1-619-930-1050
Trading Techniques	Advanced G.E.T.	1-216-645-0077
TrendSetter Software	Personal Analyst	1-800-825-1852
Ward Systems Group, Inc.	NeuroShell	1-301-662-7950

168

APPENDIX F—FUTURES CONTRACT INFORMATION

Sym	Description	Exchg	Price Scale	Daily Limit	Point Value	Min. Move	Open Time	Close Time	F	G	H	J	K	M	N	Q	U	V	X
AD	Australian Dollar (IMM)	CME	1/10000		10	1	08:20	15:00			x		x				x		
AG	Silver 1000 oz	CBOT	1/10	500	1	1	08:25	02:25		x	x			x		x	x		
AL	Aluminum	CEC	1/10	500	400	5	09:30	02:15			x	x		x		x			
BC	Major Market Index	CBOT	1/100		2.5	5	09:15	16:15	x	x	x	x	x	x	x	x	x	x	x
BO	Soybean Oil	CBOT	1/100	100	6	1	10:30	14:15	x		x		x		x	x	x		x
BP	British Pound (IMM)	CME	1/10000	500	6.25	1	08:20	15:00			x			x			x		
BR	Broiler Chickens	CME	1/100	150	4	2.5	10:10	14:00						x	x	x	x		x
C	Corn	CBOT	1/8	80	6.25	2	10:30	14:15			x		x		x		x		
CC	Cocoa	CEC	1	88	10	1	09:30	14:15			x		x		x		x		
CD	Canadian Dollar (IMM)	CME	1/10000	75	10	1	08:20	15:00			x			x			x		
CI	Consumer Price Index	CEC	1/100		10	1	09:30	14:30	x			x						x	
CL	Crude Oil (Light)	CEC	1/100	100	10	1	09:45	15:10	x	x	x	x	x	x	x	x	x	x	x
CP	Copper	CEC	1/100	500	2.5	5	09:50	14:00	x		x		x	x	x	x	x	x	x
CR	CRB Index (Large)	CEC	1/100		5	5	09:45	14:45			x		x		x		x		
CT	Cotton #2	CEC	1/100	200	5	1	10:30	14:40			x		x		x			x	
DD	Dollar/Deutsche Mark Diff	CME	1/10000		25	1	08:20	15:00			x			x			x		
DM	Deutsche Mark (IMM)	CME	1/10000	100	12.5	1	08:20	15:00			x			x			x		
DP	Dollar/British Pound Diff	CME	1/10000		25	2	08:20	15:00			x			x			x		
DR	Int'l Market Index	CEC	1/100	3000	2.5	1	09:30	16:15	x	x	x	x	x	x	x	x	x	x	
DX	US Dollar Index	CEC	1/100	500	5	1	24 hr				x			x			x		
DY	Dollar/Japanese Yen Diff	CME	1/10000		25	1	08:20	15:00			x			x			x		
EC	European Currency Unit	CME	1/100		10	1	10:00	16:05	x	x	x	x	x	x	x	x	x	x	x
ED	Eurodollar (IMM)	CME	1/100		25	1	08:20	15:00			x			x			x		
EM	London Inter-Bank Rate (IMM)	CME	1/32	150	31.25	1	08:00	15:00	x	x	x	x	x	x	x	x	x	x	x
EU	European Currency Unit	CEC	1/100		10	1	08:00	14:40			x			x			x		
FC	Cattle, Feeder	CME	1/100	150	4.4	2.5	10:05	14:00	x		x	x				x	x	x	
FF	30 Day Interest Rate	CBOT	1/32	150	31.25	1	08:00	15:00	x	x	x	x	x	x	x	x	x	x	x
FM	Misc. FM	CME	1/100	50	1	1	10:00	16:05			x			x			x		
FR	French Franc (IMM)	CME	1/10000	500	2.5	5	08:20	15:00			x			x			x		
FV	Treasury Notes 5-Yr	CBOT	1/32	96	15.625	1	08:20	15:00			x			x			x		
FY	Treasury Notes 5-Yr	CEC	1/32		15.625	1	08:20	15:00	x	x	x	x	x			x	x	x	x
GC	Gold	CEC	1/10	250	10	1	08:20	14:30		x		x		x		x		x	
GD	Gold	CME	1/10		10	10	08:20	15:00	x		x		x		x				
GH	Gold	CBOT	1/10	500	10	1	08:20	14:40		x		x		x		x		x	
GM	GNMA	CBOT	1/32	96	31.25	1	08:20	15:00			x			x			x		
GN	Gold	CME	1/10		3.32	10	08:20	15:00			x			x		x			
GS	Grain Sorghum	KCBOT	1/10	120	6.25	1	10:30	14:15			x		x			x			
HF	High Fructose Corn Syrup	MGE	1/100	100	4.8	1	10:00	14:20			x		x			x			
HG	Copper-high grade	CEC	1/100		2.5	1	09:25	14:00	x	x	x	x	x	x	x	x	x	x	x
HO	Heating oil	CEC	1/10000	200	4.2	1	09:50	15:05	x	x	x	x	x	x	x	x	x	x	x
HU	Unleaded Gas	CEC	1/10000	200	4.2	1	09:50	15:10	x	x	x	x	x	x	x	x	x	x	x
JB	Japanese Gov't Bonds	CBOT	1/100	96	31.25	1	08:00	15:00			x			x			x		
JM	Misc. JM	CME	1/100	50	1	1	10:00	16:05			x			x			x		
JO	Orange Juice	CEC	1/100	500	1.5	5	10:15	14:15			x		x			x		x	
JY	Japanese Yen (IMM)	CME	1/10000	100	12.5	1	08:20	15:00			x			x			x		
KC	Coffee	CEC	1/100	400	3.75	1	09:15	13:58			x		x		x		x		
KE	Euro-Diff Coffee	CEC	1/100	10000	3.75	1	09:00	13:58			x		x		x		x		
KI	Gold	CBOT	1/10		3.215	1	08:20	14:40		x		x		x		x		x	
KV	Value Line Index	KCBOT	1/100		5	5	09:30	16:15			x		x			x			
KW	Wheat	KCBOT	1/8	160	6.25	2	10:30	14:15			x		x		x		x		
LB	Lumber, random length	CME	1/10	50	16	1	10:00	14:05	x		x		x		x		x		x
LC	Cattle, Live	CME	1/100	150	4	2.5	10:05	14:00		x		x		x		x		x	
LG	Propane	CEC	1/100	100	4.2	1	09:40	15:05							x	x	x	x	
LH	Hogs, Live	CME	1/100	150	4	2.5	10:10	14:00		x		x		x	x	x		x	
MB	Municipal Bonds	CBOT	1/32	96	31.25	1	08:20	15:00			x			x			x		
MS	Misc. MS	CME	1/100	50	1	1	10:00	16:05			x			x			x		
MV	Mini Value Line Index	KCBOT	1/100	1500	1	5	09:30	16:15			x		x			x			
MW	Wheat, Hard Red Spring	MGE	1/8	1000	6.25	2	10:30	14:15			x		x		x		x		
NG	Natural Gas	CEC	1/1000	100	10	1	09:20	15:10	x	x	x	x	x	x	x	x	x	x	x
NK	Nikkei Index	CME	1	3000	5	5	09:30	16:15			x			x			x		

Sym	Description	Exchg	Price Scale	Daily Limit	Point Value	Min. Move	Open Time	Close Time	F	G	H	J	K	M	N	Q	U	V	X	Z
NR	Rice, CRCE (Rough)	MIDAM	1/10	30	2	1	10:15	14:30	x		x		x				x			x
NW	Wheat, White	MGE	1/8	250	6.25	2	10:30	14:15			x		x		x		x			x
O	Oats	CBOT	1/8	48	6.25	2	10:30	14:15			x		x		x		x			x
OM	Oats	MGE	1/8	80	6.25	1	10:30	14:15			x		x		x		x			x
PA	Palladium	CEC	1/100	600	1	5	08:10	14:20			x			x			x			x
PB	Pork Bellies	CME	11/100	200	4	2.5	10:10	14:00		x	x		x		x	x				
PL	Platinum	CEC	1/10	200	5	1	08:20	14:30	x	x	x	x	x	x	x	x	x	x	x	x
PN	Propane Futures	CEC	1/100	200	4.2	1	09:15	15:00	x	x	x	x	x	x	x	x	x	x	x	x
RA	Russell 3000 Index	NYFE	1/100		5	1	09:15	16:10			x			x			x			x
RF	Residual Fuel Oil	CEC	1/100	100	10	1	06:45	12:10	x	x	x	x	x	x	x	x	x	x	x	x
RT	Russell 2000 Index	NYFE	1/100		5	1	09:15	16:10			x			x			x			x
RU	Russell 3000 Index	NYFE	1/100		5	1	08:50	16:30	x		x	x	x	x	x	x	x	x	x	x
S	Soybeans	CBOT	1/8	240	6.25	2	10:30	14:15	x		x		x		x	x			x	
SB	Sugar #11	CEC	1/100	50	11.2	1	10:00	13:43			x		x		x		x	x		x
SE	Sugar #14	CEC	1/10	50	11.2	1	09:40	13:43	x		x		x		x		x	x		
SF	Swiss Franc (IMM)	CME	1/10000	150	12.5	1	08:20	15:00			x			x			x			x
SI	Silver	CEC	1/10	1000	5	1	08:25	14:25			x		x		x		x			x
SM	Soybean Meal	CBOT	1/10	100	10	1	10:30	14:15	x		x		x		x	x	x	x		x
SP	S&P 500 Index	CME	1/100	3000	5	5	09:30	16:15			x			x			x			x
SV	Silver 5000 oz	CBOT	1/10	500	5	1	08:25	14:15	x			x			x			x		x
TB	Treasury Bills 90 day (IMM)	CME	1/100	60	25	1	08:20	15:00			x			x			x			x
TG	Mortgage-Backed 9.0%	CBOT	1/32	96	31.25	1	08:20	15:00	x	x	x	x	x	x	x	x	x	x	x	x
TH	Mortgage-Backed 9.5%	CBOT	1/32	96	31.25	1	08:20	15:00	x	x	x	x	x	x	x	x	x	x	x	x
TU	Treasury Notes 2-Yr	CBOT	1/32	50	15.625	1	08:20	15:00			x			x			x			x
TW	Treasury Notes 2-Yr	CEC	1/32	50	15.625	1	08:20	15:00	x	x	x	x	x	x	x	x	x	x	x	x
TX	Topixd Stock Index	CBOT	1/10	3000	5	5	09:15	16:15			x			x			x			x
TY	Treasury Notes 10-Yr	CBOT	1/32	64	31.25	1	08:20	15:00			x			x			x			x
UB	Treasury Bonds	NYFE	1/32	96	31.25	1	08:20	16:15			x			x			x			x
US	Treasury Bonds	CBOT	1/32	96	31.25	1	08:20	15:00			x			x			x			x
W	Wheat	CBOT	1/8	160	6.25	2	10:30	14:15			x		x		x		x			x
WS	Sugar, White	CEC	1/10		0.5	1	09:45	13:45	x		x		x		x		x			
XB	Treasury Bonds	MIDAM	1/32	64	15.625	1	08:20	16:15			x			x			x			x
XC	Corn	MIDAM	1/8	80	1.5625	2	10:30	14:30			x		x		x		x			x
XD	Canadian Dollar	MIDAM	1/10000	75	5	1	08:20	15:15			x			x			x			x
XE	Soybean Meal	MIDAM	1/10	100	2	1	10:30	14:30	x		x		x		x	x	x	x		
XF	Swiss Franc	MIDAM	1/10000	150	6.25	1	08:20	15:15			x			x			x			x
XG	Copper	MIDAM	1/100	50	1	1	08:20	14:40	x	x	x	x	x	x	x	x	x	x	x	x
XH	Hogs, Live	MIDAM	1/100	150	1.5	1	10:10	14:15		x			x	x	x	x		x		x
XJ	Japanese Yen	MIDAM	1/10000	100	6.25	1	08:20	15:15			x			x			x			x
XK	Gold	MIDAM	1/10	500	3.32	1	08:20	14:40	x	x	x	x	x	x	x	x	x	x	x	x
XL	Cattle, Live	MIDAM	1/100	150	2	1	10:05	14:15		x		x		x		x		x		x
XM	Deutsche Mark	MIDAM	1/10000	100	6.25	1	08:20	15:15			x			x			x			x
XO	Oats	MIDAM	1/8	48	1.5625	2	10:30	14:30			x		x		x		x			x
XP	British Pound	MIDAM	1/10000	5	3.125	2	08:20	15:15			x			x			x			x
XS	Soybean	MIDAM	1/8	240	1.5625	2	10:30	14:30	x		x		x		x	x			x	
XT	Treasury Bills	MIDAM	1/100		12.5	1	08:20	15:15			x			x			x			x
XU	Platinum	MIDAM	1/10	65	2.5	1	08:20	14:40	x	x	x	x	x	x	x	x	x	x	x	x
XW	Wheat	MIDAM	1/8	200	1.5625	2	10:30	14:45			x		x		x		x			x
XY	Silver	MIDAM	1/10		1	1	08:25	14:40	x	x	x	x	x	x	x	x	x	x	x	x
YX	NYSE Composite Index	NYFE	1/100		5	5	09:30	16:15			x			x			x			x

BIBLIOGRAPHY

Achelis, Steven B. *Technical Analysis from A to Z.* Probus Publishing, 1995.

Appel, Gerald. *The Moving Average Convergence-Divergence Method.* Great Neck, NY: Signalert, 1979.

Babcock, Bruce Jr. *Profitable Commodity Futures Trading from A to Z.* CTCR. 1994.

Balsara, Nauzer J. *Money Management Strategies for Futures Traders.* John Wiley & Sons, Inc., 1992.

Band, Richard E. *Contrary Investing.* Penguin Books, 1985.

Bernstein, Jacob. *Cyclic Analysis in Futures Trading.* John Wiley & Sons, 1988.

Bernstein, Jacob. *Short-Term Trading in Futures.* Probus Publishing Company, 1987.

Boroson, Warren. *Mutual Fund Switch Strategies & Timing Tactics.* Probus Publishing Company, 1991.

Browne, Harry. *Why the Best-Laid Investment Plans Usually Go Wrong.* William Morrow and Company, Inc., 1987.

Carolan, Christopher. *The Spiral Calendar. New Classics Library*, 1992.

Dorsey, Thomas J. *Point & Figure Charting.* John Wiley & Sons, Inc. 1995.

Dreman, David. *The New Contrarian Investment Strategy.* Random House. 1980.

Ehlers, John F. *MESA and Trading Market Cycles.* John Wiley & Sons, Inc., 1992.

Eng, William F. *The Technical Analysis of Stocks, Options & Futures.* Probus Publishing, 1988.

Epstein, Charles B. *Managed Futures in the Institutional Portfolio.* John Wiley & Sons, Inc., 1992.

Faulker, Charles. *NLP: The New Technology of Achievement.* William Morrow and Company, Inc., 1994.

Frost, A.J. & Robert Prechter. *Elliott Wave Principle.* New Classics Library, Inc., 1985.

Graham, Benjamin. *The Intelligent Investor.* Harper & Row, 1973.

Krutsinger, Joe. *The Trading Systems ToolKit.* Probus Publishing Co., 1994.

Lofton, Todd. *Getting Started in Futures.* John Wiley & Sons, 1989.

Mancuso, Joseph R. *How to Prepare and Present a Business Plan.* Prentice Hall Press, 1983.

Maurice, S. Charles, Owen R. Phillips and C.E. Ferguson. *Economic Analysis—Theory and Application.* Richard D. Irwin, Inc., 1982.

McMillan, Lawrence G. *Options as a Strategic Investment.* New York Institute of Finance, 1986.

Nison, Steve. *Japanese Candlestick Charting Techniques.* New York Institute of Finance, 1991.

Pardo, Robert. *Design, Testing and Optimization of Trading Systems.* John Wiley & Sons, Inc.1992.

Salvatore, Dominick and Eugene A. Diulio. *Schaum's Outline of Theory and Problems of Principles of Economics.* McGraw-Hill, Inc., 1980.

Shimizu, Seiki. *The Japanese Chart of Charts.* Tokyo Futures Trading Publishing Co., 1986.

Slavin, Stephen L. *Economics: A Self-Teaching Guide.* John Wiley & Sons, Inc. 1988.

Stewart, James B. *Den of Thieves.* Simon & Schuster, 1991.

Stoken, Dick A. *Strategic Investment Timing.* Probus Publishing Co., 1990.

The Editors of *Money. Money Guide. The Stock Market.* Andrews, McMeel & Parker, 1987.

Thomsett, Michael C. *Getting Started in Options.* John Wiley & Sons, Inc., 1989.

Toppel, Edward Allen. *Zen in the Markets.* Samurai Press, 1992.

Vince, Ralph. *Portfolio Management Formulas.* John Wiley & Sons, Inc., 1990.

Wilder, J. Welles, Jr. *New Concepts in Technical Trading Systems.* Hunter Publishing Co. 1978.

GLOSSARY

Account Executive (AE)

The person who is in charge of your brokerage account.

Advance-Decline Line

Each day's number of declining issues is subtracted from the number of advancing issues. The net difference is added to a running sum, if the difference is positive or subtracted from the running sum, if the difference is negative.

Annuity

A contract where the buyer (annuitant) pays a sum of money to receive regular payments for life or a fixed period of time

Arbitrage

The simultaneous purchase and sale of two different, but closely related items to take advantage of a disparity in their prices.

Arms Equivolume

A charting method, developed by Richard Arms, wherein the width of the body represents the day's volume, while the vertical height represents the price. Simply stated, the wider the body, the greater the volume.

Arms Index

See TRIN.

Artificial Intelligence

The field of computer science dedicated to producing programs which attempt to mimic the processes of the human brain.

Associated Person (AP)

An individual who solicits orders, customers, or customer funds (or who supervises persons so engaged) on behalf of an FCM, IB, CTA, or CPO.

At-the-Money

An option whose strike price is nearest the current price of the underlying deliverable.

Average Annual Return

The rate of return which, if compounded over the duration of the track record, would yield the cumulative gain or loss actually produced during that period.

Average Directional Movement Index (ADX)

A technical indicator developed by J. Welles Wilder, which measures a market's trend intensity.

Back-end Load

The fee paid when withdrawing money from a fund.

Back Month

The contract month with the furthest expiration in the future, as opposed to the spot, or current month.

Back-Testing

The process of testing a trading strategy on historical data.

Bankers' Acceptances (BAs)

Short-term, non-interest-bearing notes sold at a discount and redeemed at maturity for full face value. Primarily used to finance foreign trade.

Basis

The difference between the price of futures and the spot price.

Basis Point

Term used to describe amount of change in yield. One hundred basis points equals 1 percent.

Bear Market

A sustained period of falling stock prices usually preceding or accompanied by a period of poor economic performance known as a recession. The opposite of a bull market.

Beta

Term used to describe the price volatility of securities. Standard & Poor's 500 Index is assigned a beta of one. Anything with a beta above one is considered to be more volatile than the Index; anything below one has less volatility than the S&P 500 Index.

Bid

An offer to purchase something at a specified price.

Boolean

A variable that may have one of only two possible values: true or false. After George Boole, English logician, credited with the invention of "Boolean logic."

Break

A very fast drop in price.

Breakaway Gap

The movement of price into a new range that leaves an area on a chart at which no trading occurred.

Breakout

The point when the market price moves out of the trend channel.

Byte

A single character of computer memory or storage

Bull Market

A stock market that is characterized by rising prices over a long period of time. The time span is not precise, but it represents a period of investor optimism, lower interest rates, and economic growth. The opposite of a bear market.

Call
> Market pre-opening consensus as to what the opening prices may be.

Call Option
> A contract that gives the buyer of the option the right, but not the obligation, to take delivery of the underlying security at a specific price within a certain time.

Call Price
> The price of a call option.

Cancel (or Straight Cancel)
> An instruction to disregard an order which you previously entered, but no longer want.

Cancel/Replace
> Instructs the broker to cancel an existing order and place instead a new order which has adjustments made in the price, action, quantity, and/or duration. You may not change the month or commodity in a cancel/replace.

Candlestick Charts
> A charting method, originally from Japan, in which the high and low are plotted as a single line and are referred to as shadows. The price range between the open and the close is plotted as a narrow rectangle and is referred to as the body. If the close is above the open, the body is white. If the close is below the open, the body is black.

C.F.T.C.
> Commodity Futures Trading Commission

Chaikin Oscillator
> Created by subtracting a 10-day EMA from a three-day EMA of the accumulation/distribution line.

Channel
> In charting, a price channel contains prices throughout a trend. There are three basic ways to draw channels: parallel, rounded and channels that connect highs or lows.

176

Clearing House

An adjunct to a futures exchange, through which transactions executed on the floor of the exchange are settled, using a process of matching purchases and sales.

Clearing Member

A member of the Clearing House. Each Clearing Member must also be a member of the Exchange. Each member of the exchange, however, need not be a member of the clearing association.

Commodity Pool Operator (CPO)

An individual or organization which operates or solicits funds for a commodity pool.

Commodity Trading Advisor (CTA)

An individual or organization who, for compensation or profit, directly or indirectly advises others as to the value of or the advisability of buying or selling futures contracts or commodity options.

Continuous Data

One long price series of data that never expires. When a current commodity month expires, the ending prices are spliced to the next front month contract and adjustments are made to the entire series of data based on the gap between the current contract and the front month. While in theory this data can be used for historical back-testing of systems, it is likely that no trades ever actually took place at these prices.

Convergence

The coming together of prices and/or indicators.

Correction

Any price reaction within the market leading to an adjustment by as 1/3 to 2/3 of the previous gain.

Cover

Purchasing back a contract which was sold earlier.

Curve-Fitting

The development of a set of complex mathematical or procedural rules which most closely approximate the known data or conditions.

Cycle

A repetitive pattern in price or time.

Day Order

An order which is to be executed, if possible, during one day only. If the order cannot be filled during the day specified, it is automatically canceled at the close.

Day Trading

Establishing and liquidating positions within one day's trading.

Derivative

A financial contract which does not necessarily have value of its own, but whose perceived value is based on the value of the underlying instrument(s).

Discretionary Account

An account for which buying and selling orders can be placed at the discretion of the broker or other designated person, without the prior consent of the account owner. The account owner signs a prior agreement granting the designated person or broker the power of attorney to place such trades.

Disregard Tape (DRT)

A DRT order is a market order which gives the floor broker the discretion to delay the execution of a market order if he believes he can execute the order at a better price by so doing. DRT orders are accepted on a "not held" basis only.

Divergence

The parting or deviation of prices and/or indicators. In technical analysis, often used to mean that technical indicators fail to corroborate or confirm one another.

Durbin-Watson Statistic

The probability that first order correlation exists. With a range of 0 and 4, the closer to 2.0, the lower the probability is.

Efficient Market Theory

The theory that all known information is already discounted by the market and reflected in the price due to market participants acting upon the information.

Elliott Wave Theory

A pattern recognition technique published by Ralph N. Elliott in 1939, which holds that the stock market follows a rhythm or pattern of five waves up with 3 waves down in a bull market and five waves down with three waves up in a bear market to form a complete cycle of eight waves.

Envelope

Lines surrounding an index or indicator - that is, trading bands.

Eurodollar

Dollars deposited in foreign banks, with the futures contract reflecting the rates offered between London branches of top US banks and foreign banks.

Evening Star Pattern

The bearish counterpart of the morning star pattern; a top reversal pattern.

Ex-Dividend Date

The date on which stock is sold without dividend. Under the five-day delivery plan, buyers of the stock on the fourth business day preceding the stockholder of record date will not receive the declared dividend.

Exercise Price

Amount for which shares can be bought or sold under the option.

Expected Months to New Peak

The average number of months between any randomly selected peak month and the subsequent month when the cumulative return will exceed the cumulative return for the selected peak month. This measure relates to futures events, but is based on historical data.

Expert Systems

Dynamic, but not adaptable, expert systems are rule-driven systems that cannot learn as the result of new information being fed into its system.

Expiration

The last day on which an option can be exercised.

Exponential Moving Average

The EMA for day i is calculated as: $A_i = aP_i + (1-a)A_{i-1}$ where P is the price on day i and a (alpha) is a smoothing constant ($0<a<1$). Alpha may be estimated as $2/(n+1)$, where n is the length of the simple moving average.

Fade

Selling a rising price or buying a falling price. For example, a trader fading an up opening would be short.

Fair Value

The theoretical price generated by an option pricing model such as Black-Scholes.

Fast Fourier Transform

A method by which to decompose data into a sum of sinusoids of varying cycle length, with each cycle being a fraction of a common fundamental cycle length.

Fill or Kill (FOK)

A Fill or Kill order instructs the broker to bid (to buy) or offer (to sell) at your specified price (which should be at or near the current market) and to immediately cancel the order if it is unable to be filled.

Floor Broker (FB)

An individual who executes any orders for the purchase or sale of any commodity futures or options contract on any contract market for any other person.

Floor Trader (FT)

An individual who executes trades for the purchase or sale of any commodity futures or options contract on any contract market for such individual's own account. Also known as a local.

Front-End Load

A sales charge for buying into a mutual fund. The sales charge typically can run as high as 4.0 to 8.5 percent and legally can be 9.0 percent or more.

Front Month

The closest month. For instance, if a futures contract expires quarterly (March, June, September and December) and it is currently August, the front month is September.

Fundamental Analysis

The analytical method by which only the sales, earnings and the value of a given tradable's assets may be considered. The theory that holds that stock market activity may be predicted by looking at the relative data and statistics of a stock as well as the management of the company in question and its earnings.

Futures Commission Merchant (FCM)

An individual or organization which does both of the following: (1) solicits or accepts orders to buy or sell futures contracts or commodity options and (2) accepts money or other assets from customers to support such orders.

Fuzzy Logic

A problem-solving method that processes inexact information inexactly.

Gap

A time period in which the range is completely above or below the previous time period's range.

GNMA (Government National Mortgage Ass'n)

US government agency whose primary function is to buy mortgages or mortgage purchase commitments and to resell them at market prices to other investors. It also designs and issues new mortgage-backed securities. Called "Ginnie Mae."

Head & Shoulders

A chart pattern often interpreted to mean a trend reversal may be imminent. A head and shoulder pattern is often associated with the topping of a market and an inverted head and shoulders is associated with the bottoming of a market. The neckline is the resistance or support area in the formation. The pattern can also be used to project prices by measuring the distance between the neckline and the head and adding that distance to the direction of the breakout if one occurs.

Hypothetical Trade

Any trade not actually executed for an account.

In-the-Money

A call option whose strike price is lower than the stock or future's price, or a put option whose strike price is higher than the underlying stock or future's price.

Intrinsic Value

The portion of an option's premium that is represented when the cash market price is greater than the exercise price.

Introducing Broker (IB)

An individual or organization that solicits or accepts orders to buy or sell futures contracts or commodity options but does not accept money or other assets from customers to support such orders.

K (as in 640K)

An abbreviation for kilobyte. A kilobyte is 1,024 bytes.

Lag
The number of data points that a filter, such as a moving average, follows or trails the input price data.

Leverage
The use of borrowed money with invested funds to increase returns. The effect is to magnify profits or losses and increase the amount of risk.

Limit
A limit order stipulates a price which the filling broker must equal or better in the execution of your order.

Limit Order
An order to buy or sell when a trade in the market occurs at a predetermined price.

Limit Up, Limit Down
Exchange restrictions on the maximum upward or downward movement permitted in the price for a commodity during any trading session.

Load
A portion of the offering price that goes toward selling costs such as sales commissions and distribution.

Local
Also called a floor trader; a member of an exchange who generally trades only for his own account, or for an account controlled by him.

Locked Limit
A market that, if not restricted, would seek price equilibrium outside the limit, but instead moves to the limit and ceases to trade.

MACD - Moving Average Convergence-Divergence
The difference between two exponentially smoothed moving averages of different length (often 12 and 24 period). Technicians often use the crossing of this value over the zero line to signal buying or selling opportunities.

Macro

A computer method commonly used in spreadsheets to automate repetitive steps by recording necessary keystrokes. The macro can then be run and the keystrokes will be implemented.

Management Fee

The amount paid to the administrator and/or management company (who may also serve as an investment advisor) for services rendered to the fund and included in the expense ratio.

Margin

In stock trading, an account in which purchase of stock may be financed with borrowed money; in futures trading, the deposit placed with the clearing house to assure fulfillment of the contract. This amount varies with market volatility and is settled in cash.

Margin Call

A demand by the lender of a margin loan that the borrower repay all or a portion of the loan.

Market if Touched (MIT)

An MIT becomes a market order if and when the market hits a price specified by you. Like limit orders, buy MITs are entered at or below the current market and sell MITs are entered at or above the current price. Unlike limit orders, there are no limitations placed on the floor broker as to fill price - he will execute your order at the best available price, the same as any market order.

Market on Close (MOC)

An MOC order is a market order which can only be filled within the closing range.

Market on Open Only (OO)

An open only order us a market order which must be executed within the official opening range of prices.

Market Order

A market order does not specify a price; rather, it instructs the filling broker to execute your order at the best price available on receipt.

Martingale

From roulette; a tactical system that requires doubling your bet after each loss, so that one win will recoup the amount you originally bet.

Mathematical Expectation

$$[(1+A)*P]-1,$$
where

P = Probability of winning, and

A = (Amt you can win) / (Amt you can lose)

Maximum Adverse Excursion

An historical measure of the maximum amount by which closed winning trades have gone against you.

Maximum Drawdown (or Largest Cumulative Decline)

The largest cumulative percentage (peak-to-valley) decline in capital of a trading account or portfolio. This measurement of risk identifies the worst-case scenario for a managed futures investment within a time period.

MB (as in 20MB)

An abbreviation for megabyte. A megabyte is 1,024 kilobytes, or roughly a million bytes.

MHz (as in 8MHz)

An abbreviation for megahertz. This is a unit of measurement for clock speed and refers to a million cycles per second. The faster the clock speed, the faster the computer.

Momentum

A time series representing change of today's price from some fixed number of days back in history.

Moving Average

A mathematical transform which is the sum of the current value plus (n-1) previous values divided by n. The result smooths fluctuations in the raw data.

Multiple Linear Regression

More than one independent variable is used to account for the variability in one dependent variable.

N.A.V. Net asset value of shares.

The total market value of an investment company's shares - securities, cash, and any accrued earnings - minus its liabilities, divided by the number of shares outstanding.

Neural Network

An artificial intelligence program that is capable of "learning" through a training process of trial and error.

Not Held

When an order is placed, often during fast market conditions, and the broker says "not held" it means that he will not be legally bound to fill the order at your price. In other words, he'll fill the order at whatever price is available.

Odd Lot

The usual amount when buying shares of stock is 100 shares (a round lot). When you buy fewer than 100 shares it is called an odd lot.

On-Balance Volume

A technical indicator consisting of a single continuous line that represents buying or selling pressure.

One-Tailed T-Test

A statistical test of significance for a distribution that changes its shape as N gets smaller; based on a variable t equal to the difference between the mean of the sample and the mean of the population divided by a result obtained by dividing the standard deviation of the sample by the square root of the number of individuals in the sample.

Options Expiration
Third Friday of the month shown

Or Better Close Only
This is a limit order which is valid only during the closing range.

Order Cancels Order (OCO)
Also called One Cancels the Other. This order consists of two separate buy or sell instructions to the filling broker who will execute whichever portion of the order he is first able to and then automatically cancel the alternate instruction.

Out of the money
The condition of a call option or warrant when the price of the underlying investment is lower than the striking price. The condition of a put option when the striking price is lower than the price of the underlying investment.

Outlier
A value removed from the other values to such an extreme that its presence cannot be attributed to the random combination of chance causes.

Overbought/Oversold Indicator
An indicator that attempts to define when prices have moved too far and too fast in either direction and thus are vulnerable to a reaction.

Overfitting
The parameters of a trading system are selected to return the highest profit over the historical data.

Over-the-Counter
The nationwide network of brokers/dealers who buy and sell securities that, for the most part, are not listed on an exchange.

Parameter
A variable, set of data, or rule that establishes a precise format for a model.

Premium

The price a buyer pays to an option writer for granting an option contract.

Program Trading

Trades based on signals from computer programs, usually entered directly from the trader's computer to the market's computer system. Since 1987 program trading is limited to times when the market is not volatile. For instance, there is a 50 point collar on the DJIA, so that no program trades may take place if the DJIA moves beyond this limit up or down in a single day's trading.

Price/Earnings Ratio (P.E.)

The price of the stock, divided by earnings per share reported over the last four quarters.

Put Option

The right, but not the obligation, to sell shares at the exercise price on or before the expiration date.

Put Price

Price of a put option.

RAM

An acronym for Random Access memory. RAM is memory that can be written to and read from, but that will only hold its contents as long as power is applied to it.

Random Walk

A theory that says there is no sequential correlation between prices from one day to the next, that prices will act unpredictably as they seek a level in response to supply and demand.

Rate of Return

According to CFTC Regulation 4.21(a)(4)(ii)(F) is calculated by dividing the net performance for the month or quarter by the net asset value at the beginning of the period.

Relative Strength Index
An indicator invented by J. Welles Wilder and used to ascertain overbought/oversold and divergent situations.

Repurchase Agreement (repo)
A financial transaction in which one party purchases securities for cash and a second party simultaneously agrees to buy them back in the future at specified terms.

Resistance
A price level at which rising prices have stopped rising and either moved sideways or reversed direction; usually seen as a price chart pattern.

R-squared
The percentage of variation in the dependent variable that is explained by the regression equation. A relative measure of fit.

Reversal Stop
A stop that, when hit, is a signal to reverse the current trading position. Also known as stop and reverse.

ROM
An acronym for Read-Only Memory. ROM is memory that can be read from, but cannot be written to. Its contents are permanent and do not require any kind of power backup.

SAR
Stop and Reverse

Saucer Base
Similar to a cup and handle formation, but the saucer base is more shallow and rounder in shape.

Secular Trend
Pertaining to a long, indefinite period of time.

Seed

The first value used to start a calculation. For example, an exponentially smoothed moving average (EMA) uses the previous day's EMA for the calculation. On the first day's calculation you could use the value of a simple moving average as the seed for the EMA.

Spike

A sharp rise in price in a single bar or two.

Spread Orders

An instruction to simultaneously buy and sell the same or related commodities in an attempt to take advantage of the price differential.

Standard Deviation

The positive square root of the expected value of the square of the difference between a random variable and its mean. The dispersion of observations from the mean observation. This measure is often expressed as a percentage on an annualized basis.

Sterling Ratio (or Return to Drawdown or MAR Ratio)

A ratio that compares the rate of return with the worst-case loss, thus a measurement or risk-adjusted rate of return, calculated as follows:
(Annual ROR) / (Maximum drawdown).

Stops

Buy stops are orders that are place at a predetermined price over the current price of the market. Sell stops are orders that are placed at a predetermined price below the current price of the market.

Stop and Reverse (SAR)

A stop that, when hit, is a signal to reverse the current trading position, from long to short or short to long. Also known as a reversal stop.

Stop Close Only (SCO)

A stop order which can be triggered and executed only during the market's closing range.

Stop Limit

A variation on the simple stop, the stop limit instructs the filling broker to fill your order at your price or better, if possible, once your stop is triggered. This gives the trader more control over his fill price. If, however, the market runs the stipulated price before the broker is able to execute it, the order becomes a regular limit order. Then, if the market does not return to the specified level before the order expires, the order will not be executed.

Stop Limit Close Only (SLCO)

A stop limit order which can be triggered and executed only during the closing range.

Stop Loss

The risk management technique in which the trade is liquidated to halt any further decline in value.

Stop with Limit

Similar to the stop limit except that the trader must stipulate two prices with the limit price being farther away from the current market than is the stop price.

Strike Price

Also known as exercise price.

Support

A historical price level at which falling prices have stopped falling and either moved sideways or reversed direction; usually seen as a price chart pattern.

T-Test

A statistical test of significance for a distribution that changes its shape as N gets smaller; based on a variable t equal to the difference between the mean of the sample and the mean of the population divided by a result obtained by dividing the standard deviation of the sample by the square root of the number of individuals in the sample.

Technical Analysis

A form of market analysis that studies supply and demand for securities and commodities based on trading price and volume studies. Using charts and modeling techniques, technicians attempt to identify price trends in a market.

Tick

The minimum fluctuation of a tradable. For example, bonds trade in 32nds, most stocks trade in eighths, S&P 500 index trades in 5 cent increments.

Trading Bands

Lines plotted in and around the price structure to form an envelope, answering whether prices are high or low and forewarning whether to buy or sell.

Transform

A process or function for changing or converting data.

TRIN

Also known as the ARMS Index. Named after its originator, Richard Arms, this volume based indicator looks at market strength and breadth and simply states whether the stocks gaining in price or those dropping in price are getting the greater share of market activity.

TRIX

Triple exponential smoothing oscillator. The one day difference of the triple exponential moving average of price.

Virus

A computer virus is a program which attaches itself to other programs and can create unexpected results on your computer.

Volatility

A measure of the degree of stability of the price of a stock, index, commodity etc. A highly volatile stock, one that experiences wide price swings, is considered to be more speculative than one with a low volatility.

Whipsaw

Losing money on both sides of a price swing.

INDEX